SHIT HAPPENS! THEN RAINBOWS

Kill Procrastination, Take Action, Live Your Dream!

DANIEL TONKIN

First published in 2017 by Daniel Tonkin
© Daniel Tonkin

The moral rights of the author have been asserted.
This book is a SpiritCast Network of Books

National Library of Australia Cataloguing-in-Publication data:

Author:
    Tonkin, Daniel
Title:
    Shit Happens! Then Rainbows;
    Kill procrastination, take action, live your dream!
ISBN-13:
    978-1978425552
ISBN-10:
    1978425554
Subjects:
    Personal Development, Business, Leadership, Success, Motivation

All rights reserved. Except as permitted under the Australian Copyright Act 1968 (for example, a fair dealing for the purposes of study, research, criticism or review), no part of this book may be reproduced, stored in a retrieval system, communicated or transmitted in any form or by any means without prior written permission. All enquiries should be made to the publisher at Daniel@shithappensthenrainbows.com.au

Editor-in-chief: *Anita Saunders*
Cover Design: *Bliss Inventive*

Disclaimer:
The material in this publication is of the nature of general comment only, and does not represent professional advice. It is not intended to provide specific guidance for particular circumstances and it should not be relied on as the basis for any decision to take action or not to take action on any matter which it covers. Readers should obtain professional advice where appropriate, before making any such decision. To the maximum extent permitted by law, the author and publisher disclaim all responsibility and liability to any person, arising directly or indirectly from any person taking or not taking action based on the information in this publication.

For Emily & Ava

For putting up with the hours I invested in researching, writing and editing while making this book come to life.

I love you both! X

Contents

Welcome vii
CHAPTER 1: Shit Happens, Then Rainbows 1
CHAPTER 2: Recognising Opportunity 13
CHAPTER 3: The Importance of Sales 27
CHAPTER 4: Supressing Emotions Got Me Nowhere 39
CHAPTER 5: What Is Your Dream? 47
CHAPTER 6: The Daniel Tonkin Creation Strategy 57
CHAPTER 7: Fuck $ 69
CHAPTER 8: Live Happily Ever After 83
Permission Granted! 91
Acknowledgments 93
About The Author 97
Contact Daniel Tonkin 99

Welcome

I was fired for sleeping on the toilet!

I'm sure you are thinking "That's just strange" or "Is that even possible?"

Well, I guess when you are as uninspired with life as I was, it's easy to switch off. After four years of study to become a fabricator, or in my words an engineer, it only took one and a half years into building my career until it was over. The interesting part was I blamed others for my misfortunes, my feelings of failure, how I was lost with life, and my anxiety.

What the fuck was wrong with me?

My journey started on February 22, 1985. Daniel John Tonkin was born. How I hated my middle name. I did like the initials DJ but that never stuck. Most people throughout my life ended up calling me Tonka; you know, like the trucks. Australians are very clever with nicknames; we remove a few letters then add an A or an O onto the end of it and there you go, a very original, creative Australian nickname! There are multiple versions like this: Jonathan—Jono, Garry—Gazza, Tonkin—Tonka; you get the gist.

Dan gets thrown around from time to time, but most people now just call me Daniel.

It makes sense as it's my name, and only took me 32 years to get back to it.

How would I best describe myself? An ordinary, successful guy!

I have failed more times than I have succeeded and have come second more times than first. I can't say I loved the feeling of failure or getting second place, but I wouldn't change it for the world.

This book is an insight into my journey up to the ripe age of 32. Together we will uncover the learnings of life through the fuck-ups, the successes, and ultimately how taking action has given me purpose. I want to share with you how business saved my life. That when times get tough, all you need is inspiration to carry you through times of despair. Inspiration can be found anywhere and at anytime, all you need to do is open your eyes. All you need to do is take action. All you need is to look inside yourself. The answers to living your best life are waiting to be unleashed, and the time is now.

Growing up I never really had any heroes. Superman, Batman, coaches: nothing really stands out in my mind. There was one sporting star that I claimed to be my favourite and maybe even a hero; his name was Laurie Daley from the Canberra Raiders who was an absolute legend of the game Rugby League, someone whom I looked up to from 10 years of age. I remember the day I bumped into him; well, I stalked him at a small shopping centre called Lanyon Marketplace where we were running a promotion for the day. It was 2010; I was now 25, in Canberra. It was my first year running my company in Sydney. I saw him from our pop-up stall and it was windy, rain falling onto my face. I decided to follow him a long way and say hello! It was awkward! As I did it he was getting into his car after a good 100-metre stalk; I imagine what he must've been thinking. *What a creep, following me to my car in the rain with a big smile, trying to shake my hand as I'm getting into my car with rain going all over my lap, steering wheel, and on my face.* I didn't really care as I had the same enthusiasm my daughter would have on Christmas Day minus the squealing when waking myself up to open the first present.

Straight after the awkward experience I was explaining it to multiple people who I met and I couldn't really explain why I was so excited to meet him, other than he was famous, I supported him as a 10-year-old, and he had achieved so much in the game—played for Australia and New South Wales which I love watching, especially the State of Origin—but my enthusiasm slowly died down. I realised I had no idea who he was, or how he achieved his success, or anything at all about him. How could he be my hero if I don't know how he created the success. He wasn't my hero after all. I just wanted to say I had one. Laurie Daley triggered something inside of me: I have never spent any time really understanding what it takes to create success. Yes, he is inspirational to many, but for me a journey to someone's success is where the true inspiration lies. I didn't have a clue what his journey was. I got so caught up in his success that I never took time to learn how he got there. I would love for my daughter, her name is Ava, by the way, to call me her hero one day. Not because I'm her dad but because of the journey we have shared.

Now with my new-found realisation one of my first real heroes that I finally put the HERO tag to was Michael Jordan and I didn't even realise this until I had the epiphany. I was inspired by his story and it gave me a feeling I had never had before: certainty/trust and belief with my journey.

I accidentally stumbled onto my new hero multiple times through the years, watching *Space Jam*, collecting his basketball cards, watching the Nike ads, reading Michael's autobiography, watching his Hall of Fame speech on YouTube, reading the many memes and watching the highlight reels amazed how he played the game. I was able to understand his story which was pivotal in my mentality with life and business. WOW! Michael Jordan, the most unlikely of choices, maybe my first hero! I found myself following and getting inspired by a journey, not by amazing destinations and huge feats.

I was only a moderate fan of basketball and the only basketball I played was with my older brother, where I could never beat him, or at school, where I could rebound but couldn't shoot. Why Michael Jordan? Well, I truly believe everyone has a great story once you take the time to understand. Learning about Michael Jordan was the first time I ever did. The MJ (Michael Jordan) brand: MJ was a basketball superstar, one of the most successful, popular, and wealthy athletes in sports history. Alongside owning basketball teams and building his own shoe brand Jordan's underneath the Nike brand.

Every story is a rag-to-riches journey; you may think I romanticised his story because of the success he created, as he was one of the first sporting stars to generate a billion dollars in revenue, and MJ being my hero may sound like the ultimate cliché, but to be honest, he was just the first person I have researched that inspired me. I love his journey more than MJ's destination. All the work, passion, and effort he put into becoming successful—that's what I loved.

The drawcard for me was finding out the reasons for the success and how the journey defined the destination. In Michael's Hall of Fame speech, he mentions Leroy Smith, who took Michael's place in the basketball team in MJ's sophomore year. How he went home and cried that night and woke up the next day and chose to work harder, he chose to act. He thanks Leroy in his speech but also says "You were wrong not to pick me" to the coach. A funny moment in the speech but so meaningful. He talks about getting cut from his team and how it motivated him to be more.

He mentions his first coach at the Chicago Bulls, Kevin Loughery, how in training they would play 5 on 5. The losing team would do sprints, often the coach would put Jordan on the losing team halfway through the game and nine out of ten times Michael's team would still win. The competitive nature drove him. It's funny how the simple parts in people's stories are what inspires me. I've used aspects of MJ's philosophy to build pillars to create my journey!

I've always loved books and stories. Strangely, I find myself enjoying reading about a person conquering challenges in life the most. Don't get me wrong, I don't like someone suffering at all, but I find I can relate to those parts of life. I never experienced much success throughout my early life, as I said before; with most things I just received a participation award. I learned to turn things around though, and make the tough times work to my advantage.

Now I knew what defined a hero I was able to create more heroes each day by simply researching and speaking to people that inspired me. Find out your parent's stories, find out your grandparent's stories, the business you're working in, your favourite musicians: there are so many great

Welcome

journeys to learn from and so many heroes to have. I'm proud to say I now have over 20 heroes, ranging from my mum, who was truly my first hero, Michael Jordan, my first coach in business, to the most recent book I've read.

Michael and the others were all also just ordinary, successful people, who have created a story that inspired me, and hopefully I can do that for you! Life, I believe, is yours to create/manifest and sometimes we just stop trying. The one aspect I got from all the stories is love the journey and only then will you be fulfilled at the destination. I loved that they all used the setbacks and the negative stories to drive them forward.

All I knew was if I was uninspired with life I was not going to help many people, including myself, so I had to be selfish and inspire myself to be truly selfless and give back. The journey I was leading was going to be a story that if I turned it into a book no one would read it, let alone be inspired from, as I wasn't inspired or engaged with my own life.

I feel my journey was a life full of participation awards and second places. To some that doesn't sound that bad. I never had the passion, drive or work habits to be number 1. I tended to blame everyone else for my outcomes, which does make sense, as how could it be my fault if I wasn't the best (sorry for the sarcasm)? I did blame others for years.

Am I a writer? No.
Have I ever considered myself a writer? Hahaha, no.
Did I ever feel I could write a book? Fuck, no.

When I finally had the balls to even look up the definition of a writer this is what I saw:
A person who has written something or who writes in a particular way. Another definition is, a person who commits his or her thoughts or ideas to writing.

I have shitloads of thoughts and ideas that I can commit to writing down, as it's better on paper than in my head! And yes, my writing will be in a particular way as it's my way.

How many dreams or great ideas play havoc in your mind? Will anyone read the book, will it make a difference, will anyone take action, am I qualified to write the book? Fear settles in then procrastination, doubt and overthinking takes over. You will never please everyone, be happy with YOU - because that will inspire others.

***

Luckily for me I tend to move to action even if it's at turtle speed, or if you had to describe it as an animal it would be a sloth as they move slower than a turtle. I can't call it procrastination as I didn't completely stop. Watching *Animal Planet,* they mention sloths move that slow moss can grow on them; hence, the initial thought of writing a book as an 11-year-old fan of *Goosebumps* took me over 10 years to make a decision to write a book. Then I finally found the people to help me move in the right direction! This isn't a fantasy horror book, I do apologise, it is a real book that is designed to get you to think then act. Yes, I'm here with no moss on me. I hope you enjoy it; the book journey has been challenging, rewarding, and life changing as I get to relive every aspect of my life.

The purpose of the book is to expand your thoughts, to open you up to slowly get you moving towards love, happiness, travel, business, fitness, health, or whatever your dreams are fulfilled by!

This book is for:

- Entrepreneurs who want to grab life by the balls and take over the world.

- People who want to enrich their lives and want to know how to make their dreams become a reality.

- Individuals who are down on their luck, have given up, or are close to giving up.

Welcome

- Anyone who is curious and happy with me dropping a few f-bombs from time to time.

I don't think there is any other quality so essential to achieve success of any kind as the quality of perseverance. During the first year of business, the Coca-Cola company sold ONLY 400 bottles of Coke! And we all know now, persistence paid off for Coca-Cola.

The success of my business today is the result of putting into practice, perseverance. Funny thing about not giving up, you learn more about you, more about people, and more about how to make success happen.

In the beginning, my business, was led by inexperience, desperation and self-doubt! Not the perfect combination to begin with but it proved to be the experience I needed from which to learn. Which has made the difference from where I was to where I am today. Often the answers we are looking for are NOT on the outside, but are within us. Turn on the light, get an aerial view of where you are and where YOU want to be in your life.

Become crystal clear on your process, crystal clear on the type of culture YOU want for your life, and lastly, become crystal clear on YOUR goals. When you do, it becomes crystal clear to your team which are the people in your life.

There are multiple ways of achieving success: you can use creativity and spend time on your own coming up with ideas, having small goals that are easy to reach, or like me which is just work your arse off, bang your head against a wall and spin multiple plates at once while they come crashing down. Then you eventually figure out how to make it work!!

From humble beginnings to incorporating my own company in August 2008. I've been fortunate to build an organisation which expands Australia and New Zealand with record sales in 2016. Turning over millions of dollars. I have also had success with opening other companies which are growing at a staggering rate. I've been able to look back on what were the key moments that helped me build a powerhouse. When I mean powerhouse, I don't just mean business. A powerhouse with everything in life which is important to me: love, family, trust, business, adventure, fitness, travel around the world, mindfulness, spirituality, relationships, learning, being a great father, a great partner/ husband-to-be, overcoming challenges, maximising the ocean, food, eating at restaurants, properties, investments, vehicles, savings, reading, movies, exercise, yoga, helping others, coaching, inspiration, travelling business class, sport, creativity, art, competitiveness, meditation, writing, fun, creating a home feel; I love going to work, I love living my life. I just chose business as the vehicle to live my life passions. For me business was important to help me engage with what I need to have a fulfilled life. Yours can be whatever you want it to be. Business saved my life, it gave me purpose, something to give a fuck about, with this new feeling I found inspiration everywhere.

This book will help you take action, as small as it may be, to help you live the life you want to live, not just dream to live! I'm a living example. It's not too late nor are you too young to achieve the impossible, which most of the time are barriers we have created. Whether you are 16, 25, 35, 65, or 85, it's not too early or too late!

I'm just an ordinary, successful guy.

Time to turn a page in your life.

CHAPTER 1

Shit Happens, Then Rainbows

Failure breeds success.

Three Feet From Gold

One of the most common causes of failure is the habit of quitting when one is overtaken by temporary defeat. Every person is guilty of this mistake at one time or another. The story of R.U. Darby and how he followed his uncle in search of gold is one that has imprinted itself in my memory.

During the gold rush days, a lot of prospectors went to search for vast riches in the ground all over the US. Darby and his uncle, like thousands of others, wanted to stake their claim. The labour was tough but the lust of gold was strong and after weeks of demanding work they were rewarded by the discovery of shining ore. They needed machinery to bring the ore to the surface. Retracing their steps back home in Williamsburg, Maryland they began looking for investors in their new venture. After rallying up enough money from friends and family to buy machinery Darby and his uncle began working on their mine.

The first car of ore mined was shipped to a smelter. The returns proved they had one of the richest mines in Colorado! A few more cars of the ore would clear debts and then the big profits would start coming in.

Just like that the vein of gold disappeared! They had come to the end of the rainbow; the pot of gold was no longer there. They drilled on desperately but couldn't trace the gold again; running short on resources, they decided to QUIT.

Selling all the machinery to a junkman for a few hundred dollars they took a train back home. The junkman decided to call a mining engineer to investigate the mine; the engineer after doing multiple calculations, advised the project had failed because the previous owners had no idea about fault lines. The calculations showed the vein of gold could be found only three feet away from where Darby had stopped drilling. That's where it was found.

The junkman took millions of dollars in ore from the mine, because he knew enough to seek expert advice before giving up.

Darby heard about his misfortune and the story imprinted into his mind. "I can't believe I was three feet away from gold and I stopped." Darby went into selling life insurance and with the three-feet-away-from-gold story ringing in his mind he never took no for an answer or thought about quitting. Darby ended up building a life insurance empire and paying back all his debt. Darby's business was generating over 100 million dollars in revenue annually and he owes this to the lesson he learned from quitting the gold business. Before rainbows come into anyone's life they are sure to find a lot of shit. When you're covered in shit, the easiest and most logical thing to do is take a shower and quit, then find something new to do. In Darby's experience the greatest of success is always found just before defeat. A quote I love is: "Tough times don't last, tough people do."

My Gold Rush Moment

In September 2012, I experienced my own three-feet-from-gold moment but mine started out like this—how I lost 100K in 10 weeks—sounds like a TV show. I had just recently upgraded offices. It was an exciting time for myself and the STM team as we had moved away from our first location on George Street in Sydney's CBD, a rundown building next to McDonald's which always had a strange aroma. We constantly had to dodge teenagers smoking in front of the office, once we slipped passed them we had to step over the homeless people sleeping on our doorstep so we could walk into the office. We moved to our new location on York Street, also in Sydney's CBD; this part of Sydney has a very different feel, everything around our new office was clean, everyone dressed in suits and we were across from the QVB. The Queen Victoria building is a must-see in Sydney, it's an architectural wonder. Happens to be the home to the biggest retailers in Australia; the rent prices are astronomical.

My first office in Sydney, on the other hand, wasn't wonderful. The George Street office not only had the smell of McDonald's but also kebabs! Next to McDonald's and above a kebab store. We would say proudly "Any food we eat in the office would have a tinge of kebab with a touch of McDonald's odour" but secretly it made us sick! Don't get me wrong, in the early days we for sure ate many kebabs in the early hours of the morning after many drinks celebrating life! But I always remembered the smell the next morning. One of those mornings I slugged my way into the office and I was waiting for the lift, which you never knew if it would arrive as the lift broke nearly on a weekly basis, and yes, I have been stuck in that lift many times. The longest was an hour. I really hoped I wasn't going to die. But considering how often it broke down, no one has died so that gave me a bit of confidence.

As I was waiting for the lift, looking at the kebab store behind me, I noticed cockroaches literally everywhere. I instantly thought, *What the fuck, why did I eat the kebab the night before!* I instantly got a sickening feeling deep in my stomach, then rushed up to the bathroom vomiting everywhere, some people convincing me it was the alcohol; I still believe to this day it was the kebab. If the smell wasn't bad enough for the office culture, you could never sneak up on anyone as the creaking in the office was so loud everyone could hear, so you always played music that would overshadow the creaking. We all have to start somewhere.

When I first arrived from Perth at the back end of 2009 I was 100% ready to take on the Sydney expansion. I felt the George Street office was the perfect place. The office didn't look good, but we created a real buzz about it, even though I had limited money and it was all I could afford, to be honest.

The time had come to move to the new York Street office, it had so much promise, it was a guaranteed success; our contracted team was bigger, we had more money, so the timing seemed perfect.

My excitement and feeling with moving into our new office on York Street was, well ... how can you say, fucking ecstatic after our experience with our first Sydney location. But as they say on *Game of Thrones,* winter was coming.

Shit will happen, then rainbows.

How to lose $100,000 in 10 weeks: how I wish that sentence was weight not money, because during this time my diet did consist of late-night take-away dinners with alcohol to wash it down, not a good recipe for a healthy, balanced life, so as you can imagine I had literally turned into a balloon and was on a personal best of 120 kg. Normally a personal best would be something to celebrate but I was fucking fat, which was an incredible effort as I was super fit only a few years before. I was a fitness freak only a few years earlier, which I would remind anyone that would listen by showing photos of a 6 pack I used to have. To be honest, I didn't even realise I had put so much weight on, I even convinced myself I looked good.

It's funny the things we try and convince ourselves about. The lies we tell ourselves and others to make ourselves feel better. Who am I?

I had focused so much on having a successful business I was failing in a lot of other areas and everything was about to come undone. My insecurities were about to show themselves. I convinced myself the white lies were for a good cause, that me disconnecting from everyone and focusing solely on business was going to fix my anxiety with life. *Maybe all the money in the world can solve my issues,* was my thought process.

Then it started to unravel in November 2012.

We received a letter from the supplier to announce they were coming to our warehouse to audit our stock. The sickness I felt in my stomach when I found out $30,000 worth of product had gone missing was overwhelming: how did this slip past me? A legal challenge needed to be resolved and cost another $20,000. I was not in a good head space so I went MIA and of course the business suffered which caused another $20,000 loss. I had just spent money getting an office set up in Brisbane and was planning to move there in January 2013. How could I leave the Sydney office in this mess? So I stayed and lost the investment, more money gone. I had a lot of contractors deciding to move on, I had employees deciding to move on, and by the end of January 2013 when the dust settled I had lost $100,000. When shit hits the fan it doesn't take long to unravel. I was left with a grand total of $0; I did have my sales force, car, and a few other investments, but the feeling of failure overwhelmed me. If I didn't get things moving everything would be gone pretty quick.

Not only was I about to lose the business, but I was also going through a breakup of a long-lasting relationship with the mother of my daughter, now ballooning at 120kg (literally a fat bastard), living a lie, pretending to be someone I wasn't because I wasn't proud of my past. Finding it hard to trust, love, protecting myself as much as I could through deceit and focusing on work. I finally hit rock bottom and had no idea what the fuck to do.

I was about to be a statistic: 80% of businesses fail in the first year, then a big portion of the rest fail in the next five years. Well, I was in my fifth year in business and fair to say it wasn't looking promising.

I had just about given up on life and business when an angel appeared: her name is Michele Jones, she is an author, coach, mentor, and friend. Mish arrived at the perfect time; she was really a lifeline.

My support network/family/friends were all in Perth. My daughter was in Brisbane so I was alone to deal with my struggles. I really did feel alone. I was asking myself "Why was I in Sydney?" and "What is the purpose of building something if there is no one around to share it with?"

I do believe everything happens for a reason so when Michele and I sat down in late January 2013 we had a very real conversation and I put it all on the table. I lie, no one wants to be around me, I'm alone, no one gets me, I'm fat, I have no money, I've lost my daughter, partner is now gone, I'm drinking alcohol daily, overeating, everyone else's fault, I don't trust neither do I love or show love, I've stopped dreaming, and forgotten about my purpose.

Michele asked calmy "Well, is that who you are? Is that what you want your life to stand for?"

It was a simple question but powerful.

Shit happens, then rainbows.

Looking back, I was full of excuses. I drew a line in the sand that day and it was the most pivotal moment in my life. I decided on how I wanted to be, how life was going to mould around me vs me mould around life and lastly I took control and got my life back. I could slightly remember the success I experienced as a 10-year-old earning the glow-in-the-dark stars, then the excitement I had as a 17-year-old deciding to train my scrawny body to build muscles, then the feeling of accomplishment opening my company as a 23-year-old. When you're down and out it takes a lot to be able to remember as those feelings seem like a lifetime ago. I wanted to get those feelings back, but it seemed so far away, impossible to attain.

How did I start? Well, simple; I put it all on the table and took small (sloth-moving slow) actions into the areas that I wanted to improve. Then have an accountability buddy like Michele to not take any shit and shut down all excuses to make sure you are moving towards your dreams.

Fuck, it was hard.

I had to be organised, which I hate, I had to plan, which I hate, I had to be honest with everyone around me about myself and the future, which I hated, I had to have systems and structures inside my business and life, which I hated, and I had to take action, which I loved.

To instill change it's simple but funny how many of us don't have a vision for our life/business/work, don't have clear checkpoints, or goals on how to live our dreams; many of us are missing the detailed plans on how to help us move to live a life of purpose. The most important part is mentors to keep you engaged, honest, and to remind you the dream is already done, you just need claim it by taking action.

By the end of 2013 I had turned my weaknesses into strengths, hates into loves as I could see the results and how I felt day to day.

That year, 2013, introduced me to three people that would change my life forever:
1. Lifelong coach and friend Michele Jones
2. Best friend and partner in business Rory Dixon
3. Love of my life Emily Visscher

Life will test you and like the phoenix, when you are destroyed you can rise bigger and better than ever.

The year ended with the $100,000 generated back into the business plus extra. Three amazing people introduced into my life so feeling good, I lost 20kgs so looking good, got back to a good routine of exercise, clean living, less alcohol, no more being alone, healthy food, trust in my life, constant visits with my daughter, a healthy relationship with my daughter's mother, love in my life and reconnecting to family and friends. Now I can actually help others as I've looked after myself, people wanted to be a part of my business again which laid the foundation to what we have created today. Without the shit in 2013 the rainbows would've never arrived in the years afterwards.

Things Will Get Tough Before They Get Good

Finally I set a long term goal based on what I wanted, versus what others thought was good for me.

I remember walking into the gym for the very first time as a skinny 17-year-old with my best friend Ryan, completely confused on what we were both supposed to do. We went straight to the bench press, it was the only equipment we knew how to use; we lifted 30 kg. Looking back it's pretty embarrassing but at the time that was a massive amount and for the next three days I could barely move my arms. I had a dream early on that I wanted to look good as I thought the cosmetic aspect was the most important part. This is where my fascination with health and fitness started. For the next four years, I went to the gym. It didn't matter if I was sick, hungover, tired, or had plans, I made sure I turned up four times a week to focus on weights and I left one day for cardio which would be boxing/bike class or a run.

I decided to become an expert and learn everything I could. I went from being a skinny 17-year-old barely lifting 30kg, with a very feminine body weighing in at 79kg; look, I'm 189 cm tall so as you can imagine I had the lanky look going on. As any teenager, male or female, being self-conscious about the way you look, the gym was a good chance at getting my confidence back, especially when you don't have the mindset or belief to work on it in other ways. Showing up to train at the gym each day when you're the youngest, skinniest person is challenging. I knew I could improve even if it was going to be a long journey and most importantly it was going to get a lot tougher before it got easier. It was easy to be motivated for the first six weeks, as that's when I had the most improvement, but then your friends are going out drinking, you get tired, birthdays come up, you drive past KFC and you're hungry which is a bad combination. You need to be clear with what you want, then be disciplined. I see so many people with all the right intentions just stop showing up, until they eventually stop going altogether, while gyms still collect their money.

For me, getting my confidence back was the purpose. I had to do something or I was going to be another sucker still paying the gym, not showing up, so I hired a personal trainer with the little money I had. At the time, I was earning a huge $160 per week so hiring a trainer at $40 an hour was a big portion of my income but I knew I needed to or I would most likely give up. Starting the gym as a 17-year-old and sticking to it with everything happening was tough but four years later as a 21-year-old I looked incredible, felt amazing. To celebrate my 21st we did a trip of a lifetime around the world with a group of close friends who were all turning 21 that year. At this time, I was weighing in at 92kg with 6-8% body fat, looking and feeling good, destination was complete and I had a new wave of confidence about me. It was an important lesson I learned about how tough things will get and how life throws so many obstacles in your way, but the feeling you will have once finally arriving at the chosen destination can't be taken away.

Looking back it seemed like a pretty basic goal and yes, maybe it was; but it taught me valuable lessons I use in life that are relevant in so many areas. It's the discipline, vision, and action you will need to commit to for a period of time to achieve any dream. Patience is key to success. I wanted to feel good and look good but it was a four-year journey; going to the gym for hours every week isn't very exciting, you make it exciting, training with friends, listening to music, and setting yourself challenges. I had to deploy patience and learn to love the boredom of showing up to train hours on end each week. This was an important skill to master as it helped me through other aspects of my life when shit gets real tough, not just gym tough. I mean, life tough; skills are transferable and what I was building was a mentality to manifest my thoughts through taking action for as long as I needed to.

Write down a victory in your life that you would want to recreate the success strategy?

What were the attributes that helped you with the victory?

What were the habits that were repeated, that enabled the victory?

Everything is always tough at the start; the bigger the goal the more time you need to allow and the more likely challenges will arise. Before embarking on any journey ask yourself this: Do you love only the victory but shy away from the fight? Do you want the reward but not the struggle? If you want greatness, success, and happiness, you need to ask yourself what pain are you willing to go through and what time frame are you prepared to invest to have the rewards, victories, and the successes?

Things you care about most are the hardest to achieve and the easiest to give up on.

Building your dream business, house, body, relationship, and life all sound like great causes but why are they so easy to give up on?

It's easy to be focused or disciplined for one day, one week, but the longer the time frame the harder it becomes and the more resources, tools you need. One month is tough but not as tough as one year, but fuck, 10 years is super tough but not compared to 20 years. Most people don't worry about or focus on anything too long as it's hard and takes time to plan. The key ingredients are deploying patience, having a plan, taking action over a period of time and coming to terms with what pain threshold you are prepared to go through.

Hey, You're Okay, You're Exactly Where You Need to Be

If you have shit in your life right now I say, "Great, you are exactly where you need to be."

If everything is amazing and there are no problems, give yourself a day, a week, or a month; something will pop up.

The wonderful thing about problems is you do get better at dealing with them, even if its only a very small step at a time. When there are multiple problems all at once, overwhelm starts to kick in. We have all been there, wanting to shout and scream at the top of your lungs for no real reason other than to let out steam, frustration on someone, something, or to the vastness of space.

We all need to start somewhere and draw the line in the sand! For me, it's been multiple times in my life; for you, maybe after this book.

Life Is About Solving Problems, Solve Your Problem

Life is about solving problems! Stop band aiding your challenges! The issues you have in your life may or may not be your fault but you, your family, your work colleagues, your friends, and all of the animals and humans on the planet don't deserve the shit you will put on yourself and others by constantly ignoring the overriding problems.

I truly believe happiness comes from solving problems. Problems are constant in life. When I solved my problem of having a lack of confidence by buying a gym membership I was creating new problems, like going to the gym, hiring a personal trainer and finding a way to fund the trainer with the minimal amount of money I had.

When I solved the problem of having a purpose by creating a vision, having checkpoints, goals, and creating a detailed plan a whole new range of problems were created, like I need to have time each week to review, I need to make sure I get hold of a mentor to keep me accountable even when I haven't done all the things I said I would and most importantly I have to do the work.

Problems never stop, they are merely exchanged or upgraded.

Happiness comes from solving problems. The keyword is "solving"; if you're avoiding your problems or feel you don't have any, you're going to make yourself unhappy. If you feel you have problems that you can't solve, again you will be unhappy. You need to solve your problems, not focus on never having problems: that's the secret.

To be happy you need to solve something. Happiness I believe is a form of action. Not something you will find reading motivational posters, from a mentor, or even from reading articles online. The answer to happiness isn't just going to pop up and appear. Once you have $100,000 saved then you will find happiness, or once you travel to 40 countries then you will find the answer to happiness. Happiness isn't a destination, it's a journey, and the answer won't be found in the ideal job, idea, or even a book.

Happiness is a work in progress because solving problems is a work in progress. Happiness will occur when you find problems you enjoy solving and enjoy having.

Sometimes the problems are simple, like I want to save money; so start off by setting up a separate account, get a weekly transfer set up, then transfer a small amount every week into the account and create a succesful habit. Other times the problems are complicated: finding a career you enjoy, fixing the relationship with your dad, or buying your first house.

Whatever the problems are, the concept is the same: solve problems and be happy. Unfortunately for many people life doesn't feel that simple. That's because they fuck things up in a few ways: either by denying the problems exist, not taking any action, ignoring the problems, or by having a victim mentality and blaming others. Don't hide from the problems, face them head on even if you only take small actions. No more Band-Aid fixes over the problems; solve them or overwhelm will kick in and unhappiness will settle in.

Shit happens, then rainbows. I love this quote. We all have our stories. Rainbows are created by the refraction and reflection of sunlight. When sunlight passes through the rain droplets, you see the beams of sunlight that are normally unnoticeable. Depending on what angle the light hits the raindrop depends on the colour of the light you get. You need a combination of rain and sunlight to see the rainbow. Even after the roughest of storms a rainbow will appear! It's a great metaphor for shit happens, then rainbows will appear! Rainbows need the rain and the sunlight to create the colours in the sky.

The rainbow always comes after the storm.

CHAPTER 2

Recognising Opportunity

What does opportunity look like?

1. Find It

I was 21, just finished my four years of fabrication "engineering" and was now on a trip of a lifetime around the world with a great bunch of friends, starting in Singapore and ending in Las Vegas. After only three weeks of visiting a handful of countries I found myself staring at the Virgin Mary hovering above my bed in a small, rundown hospital. I was in party paradise, Mykonos, Greece, unable to party.

It all started coming home from a beach bar early one morning, motoring on the hire scooter. I remember the white dusty long road which took us back to our accommodation. I was riding down a steep hill, turning too fast around a bend, and then I tried to slow down, but the bike went straight into the wall with a "BANG"; that's the last thing I can remember hearing before I came back to consciousness. Upon regaining consciousness, there was dust everywhere and all I could hear was a wide range of languages being spoken around me. The voices sounded urgent and stressed; looking up, there was a circle of people looking at me! I was sprawled across the dusty ground, the motorbike 10 metres away from me! My next thought was *FUCK, I messed up;* all of a sudden, I could recognise one voice in the crowd and it was my best friend, Brenden. I felt relieved but once I worked out what he was saying instantly the panic rushed in. All I can remember him saying was, "Don't close your eyes" and "Don't die". I was like, fuck, something is seriously wrong, and when I looked down, blood was everywhere. If only I had chosen to wear proper clothing, not thongs, shorts, and a singlet. Finally, an ambulance-looking vehicle arrived and gave me a lot of morphine for the pain and then I was off to the hole in the wall they called a hospital.

I lay in my bed, looking towards the ceiling, waiting for my operation, and then emergency transport to Athens which was a plane ride away, where I would see the specialised doctors as my injuries were serious. As I patiently waited, The Virgin Mary appeared hovering above me; I've never been a religious man but I believe everything happens for a reason. The morphine may be to blame but it dawned on me that today wasn't my time to die. Time to go to the operating theatre, to fix me up as much a possible before I travel, my first of many surgeries to stitch up the massive gash in my arm, close up the hole in my knee, and then attempt to save my foot and get ready for the operation in Athens by the experts, as due to the severity of my injury only a few surgeons in Athens could successfully do it.

Arriving at the Mykonos airport I was feeling numb, shocked, I was still in disbelief about what had happened and I couldn't imagine the pain I would feel inside if I was to lose my foot. I arrived at the airport; the hospital staff lowered me into a wheelchair, pushed me through the airport, and then carried me onto the plane. I'm sprawled over three seats to keep my foot elevated as the doctors said it was imperative to keep my foot from dying. I was welcomed at Athens airport by ambulance officers that had the sirens blaring all the way to the Athens emergency department. I was taken straight to an operating room, where I had a team of doctors around me discussing my injury, I had no idea what they were saying as they were speaking Greek. I assumed it was bad as no one was talking to me, all the doctors walked off except one, and with a thick Greek accent he done his best to try and explain what was happening. I went into a trance; all I remember him saying is I will do everything in my power to keep your foot.

When I woke up I saw familiar faces as my friends whom I travelled with were in the room. The first question I asked was, "Is my foot still attached?" They all answered with enthusiasm, "Yes, it was, the doctors managed to keep it on for now." I didn't question the now part as I was just glad to see familiar faces, it even put a slight smile on my face seeing my friends again. I knew they were continuing their travels soon and I was going to be in the hospital for weeks alone until I was well enough to travel back home to Perth. Those weeks felt like months. I was lonely, in pain every hour; I was ready to go back home.

After weeks in hospital in Greece I was finally released; what a relief. It was time to fly back to Perth, Australia. I was met at the airport by Mum and a previous girlfriend; I had tears of joy, I was happy to be alive and back to reality. I was only home for a day when my nightmare started again and I had to be rushed to hospital as my foot was badly infected. Again, I was close to losing my foot and had to be in hospital for weeks; the doctors said it would heal eventually but not for the next year. I had a lot of free time on my hands. Back in Perth I felt different: bored, lost, unsure, uninspired, and in this condition, unemployable. It took months before I could get back to work and years before I fully healed.

I had feelings of despair, I finally reached rock-bottom. I wasn't going out, I couldn't train at the gym, my relationship with my girlfriend at the time broke down. I couldn't understand, after not dying and surviving, why was I left feeling like this, what was it all for? I stumbled upon Michael Jordan's story on the internet; I knew a bit about him as I had his basketball cards, I watched *Space Jam*, but I never watched/read anything about his story so I was curious to know more. My research continued, I was hooked at that point to change my life and I decided to use the time of healing to re-educate myself and learn a new way of thinking as MJ had an outlook on life that made him seem invincible. I wanted to create my story, one where people would listen and get the same feelings I had listening to MJ's. It's interesting what happens when opportunity presents itself and you say YES; maybe Michael Jordan was always meant to kick-start my curiosity, as every now and again he would somehow appear in my life through basketball cards, movies, memes.

I began my fascination with stories and wanted to know how people lived amazing lives and what led them to their dreams, so I began with the stories of Will Smith, then continued with many more: a few examples are Richard Branson, Mahatma Gandhi, Phil Knight, and the Red Hot Chili Peppers lead singer Anthony Kiedis. Every story was unique but all had the same principles. They all wanted to create something from nothing and had an urge to make it work no matter what others said.

I believe this is where my journey truly started. After months of recovering I finally got back to work even though I knew something was missing. I wanted to do something but I had no vehicle and I was still fearful of change, so I decided to take small action and leave the big fabrication company in pursuit for another opportunity in a smaller boutique type company, and hoped that would help the emptiness I was feeling inside. I was still unsure on leaving the engineering industry as I was too scared. I started working at a small engineering business; I still had the same feelings in the back of my mind but I had invested so much time, so why leave the industry? After the move, I was left wondering, what next? I knew I had to change careers but I didn't know where to look. I was concerned about leaving an industry I had spent years mastering.

2. Saying "YES"

A friend of mine introduced me to a network marketing business called ACN in 2006; it was my first taste at running a small business. I was unsure, but needing a change I said YES; a lot of people said no. It was an opportunity I could do alongside my engineering career; it revitalised me and was only going to take up a small amount of time with a small initial investment. Shortly after a friend introduced me to my first mentor, Farid Lerno. Working with Farid was when I decided I could be an entrepreneur. He had a unique gift in explaining what will happen if you don't take a chance. He was living a life that looked impressive; he reminded me of a real-life story of what the autobiographies I was reading. He worked from home, had property in a few areas, I felt this is where I would want to spend my life. You realise you don't need anything special, just determination and grit. I loved the idea of building something from nothing; I had feelings of purpose, drive, and ambition for the first time since I was 17 deciding to train at the gym. I achieved a lot quickly; my team grew to 20 in a short amount of time, I earned the initial investment back through the income I generated, and now I was earning extra income on top. I loved what network marketing taught me; it was time to get my own brand on the wall. The experience gave me the vision I needed to move me forward. I'm so glad I said YES, it allowed me to then say YES to the next opportunity as I was now ready.

In mid-2007, the next phone call was from another friend from school; he called about a sales opportunity. I was recently fired from my engineering career from, yes, sleeping on the toilet, so I was unemployed, with nothing to lose. I had experience in network marketing, I was reading a lot of books looking for my next idea, I knew there were gaps I needed to close. Communication alongside the art of sales was spoken about from research I was doing as the number one skill you must master to give yourself a chance in building a business and being an entrepreneur. So I thought, why not? It's a YES. Working sales solely on commission is tough and yes, there were days I wanted to go back to my old career as it was a safe option and income guaranteed; most people wouldn't think working purely based on commission, doing sales, was an opportunity in the first place. I knew I needed to master the skills to move into the person I needed to become to grow my future businesses.

My career in sales was like a roller coaster. The ups were incredible—there were weeks I earned $2000—and the downs were also terrible where there were weeks where I only earned $200; I couldn't afford rent. Who knew saying yes to an opportunity was going to be this tough—I needed guidance. The timing was perfect; that's when I met my second mentor, Darren Wright. I was fortunate; he saw potential in me even though I wasn't the easiest prodigy. I didn't listen, I showed up to our meetings late, I was disorganised, I argued wherever possible, and this reflected in my results. After one year working alongside Darren and learning all the skills needed to run a successful company, I opened my company STM International in August 2008, a sales and marketing business that specialised in sales solutions. My name finally on the wall, with people that were committed day and night, ready to build something from nothing, to create a legacy and a vision!

I now had a new lease on life! I feel business saved my life and gave me a purpose, focus, passion, vision, and feelings I've never experienced.

As a 23-year-old my goals were simple: have $100K saved, buy a house, and take over the world.

For me it's not so much about recognising opportunity because who would be able to recognise a phone call about a network marketing business would lead me to open my own company?

I believe it's about saying **YES** to opportunity as that's the key to opening new doors. Through me saying yes it made me more curious; I stopped saying no and looked at reasons why I could say yes. When opportunity presents itself, it could be in so many forms, like an opportunity to step up at work, a surprise request from a friend, or any type of unfamiliar challenge. You will never know unless you give it a go. If you are someone that says no more often than yes and wants to change that, there is something you can do. I find sometimes the people closest to us are the biggest naysayers; they love a good no. It's because they care about us and know us for our flaws and positives. Fear is a massive killer to people saying yes. My principles are simple: is the person I'm asking an expert in the area I want information on? Expert, I mean, is currently having success in that area. For example, if you are contemplating starting a company, go seek someone who is currently running a successful company for advice versus your friend who has just got their first job. If you're asking relationship advice ask the person who has been happily married versus a friend who is single and out partying each Saturday night until five a.m.

There is advice everywhere, wanted or not wanted. Be wary of who is giving you advice; are they qualified or are they being openly negative? Don't overthink it and before you say no, look at every option to say yes. Yes, I'm talking about the smallest of things, not only the biggest of opportunities. You're at home, your partner suggests you cook; instead of arguing it could be an amazing opportunity to learn something about food and become the next MasterChef. Maybe not MasterChef but you now have a great dish you now can prepare whenever, its a talking point when you see your friends and family next. You could find a passion with cooking which I found once I gave it a go, did the research, and created some great dishes; now it's a passion when before it was a task.

Sir Richard Branson is someone that was so passionate about saying **YES to opportunity** and then finding ways to make it happen. I love this quote from the Virgin founder:

"If somebody offers you an amazing opportunity but you are not sure you can do it, say yes—then learn how to do it later!"

Yes creates opportunity. So often we are afraid of life—we fear failure, we anticipate the worst, we don't know what to expect. In doing so and often by saying "no" to opportunities, we reject many of life's opportunities.. Anything that creates curiosity within us or that generates some desire to guide us to a yes, maybe you need to learn more.

We let our fears, instead of our creativity and love, guide us and rationalise a "no." I have seen it hundreds of times. Typically, people who say "no" to opportunity love to convince you (or themselves?) why it was the right choice for a list of reasons. I am here to say, yes can often be right! Deep down, we know when it is.

By saying yes, we often need to say no to others. This is not about being a "yes person" or feeling pressured to do things we don't want to do. It's about having the courage and conviction to do the things we know we really want to do. So much so sometimes they scare us.

Six reasons to say YES

1. Yes opens doors

Opportunity sometimes knocks gently and does not wait for perfect timing. The truth is—there is no perfect timing! When we say no, we reject more than the opportunity, we reject the fun it brings, what it teaches us if we don't allow the initial yes. **Yes leads to more doors, no closes them.**

2. Someone believes you can

If someone presents you with an opportunity, they must see the value you can contribute. Before saying no take into consideration the fact that they wouldn't have approached you if they didn't have trust in you.

3. Opportunities do not always come again

Life and luck favour the bold. Don't let fear of failure stop you from making an educated decision. By educated, I mean by researching and asking the right people, not your couch critics.

4. It attracts positivity

The word itself is inviting and empowering. It is like saying, "World, I got this!"

Life is richer, fuller, more vibrant. When we say yes to things that matter to us, we do more, create more, live more.

5. Push yourself

Why are we all here if not to get the most out of our lives? By saying yes, we invite possibility into our lives and the ability to learn what we are capable of and see just how far we can go.

6. Life is short. Ask not why, but why not?
One of my favourite Steve Jobs quotes is: "Remembering that I'll be dead soon is the most valuable tool I've ever encountered to help me make big choices in life." A little perspective helps us abandon our fears while we are above ground.

3. The Grass Is Greener Where You Water It (Cultivate It)

Once you do say YES don't be distracted by the shiny objects that will come your way, this is where discipline comes into play.

The next story is one that reminds us of the importance of staying on your path even when you're unsure if it's leading anywhere.

Chinese Bamboo Tree

I love the story of the Chinese bamboo tree:

Like any plant, growth requires nurturing—water, fertile soil, sunshine. First you need to plant the small seed, water it, fertilise it, and make sure there is plenty of sunlight; after one year there are no visible signs of growth. In the second year again repeat the process and still nothing happens. Year three and four comes around, still applying the same process, and yet nothing has happened, no growth above the soil. Our patience is tested and we begin to wonder if our efforts will ever be rewarded. This is when you question your journey. Is it worth it?

The fifth year you continue the process with water and fertilising the seed and then—take note. Sometime during the fifth year, the Chinese bamboo tree sprouts and grows between EIGHTY TO NINETY FEET IN SIX WEEKS!

Life is like the growing process of the Chinese bamboo tree.

It is often frustrating. We work hard and do the right things, still nothing happens. For those who do the right things, who aren't discouraged with the shit that will happen first before the rainbow, and are sure, things will happen. Finally, begin to receive the rewards.

Often the rewards from seeds that were planted take years to harvest.

As nothing was happening on the surface underneath the tree was growing a foundation that would support the future growth of the bamboo tree. The same principle is true for people. People who patiently take small actions towards worthwhile dreams and goals, building strong character while overcoming adversity and challenges, are laying a foundation for growth in their lives. Had the Chinese bamboo tree farmer dug up his little seed every year to see if it was growing, he would have stunted the Chinese bamboo tree's growth.

Can we stay focused and continue to believe in what we are doing even when we don't see immediate results? In a culture driven by instant gratification—this is our biggest challenge.

I hear the saying being used everywhere: remember to "Keep trying! and NEVER give up!" The change may be slow—even invisible at times—but suddenly, as in the case of the Chinese bamboo tree, we will surprise ourselves.

We live in a quick-fix society. We get frustrated if we must wait more than a few seconds for the internet to give us access to Facebook or get stuck in traffic jams for lengthy periods of time. We want instant solutions to every complex problem. We want it all now!

One thing is required: belief! The growers of the Chinese bamboo tree have faith that if they keep nurturing the plant, it will succeed. Well, you must have the same kind of belief in your bamboo tree, whether it is to run a successful business, live a purposeful life, raise well-adjusted children, or earn extra income to spend on yourself. You must have belief that if you keep taking small actions building your business, creating your vision for your life, honing your craft, reading to your children, having a budget, or maybe getting an extra job, then you too will see rapid growth in the future.

This is the hard part for most of us. We get so excited about the idea that's been planted inside of us that we simply can't wait for it to blossom. Therefore, within days or weeks of the initial planting, we become frustrated and begin to second guess ourselves, or worse, quit.

Sometimes, in our doubt, we dig up our seed and plant it elsewhere, in hopes that it will quickly grow in more fertile ground. We see this happen with people who change jobs every year in the pursuit of greener pastures. More often than not, these people are greatly disappointed when their Chinese bamboo tree doesn't grow any faster in the new location.

Other times, people will water the ground for a time but then quickly become frustrated. They start to wonder if it's worth all of the effort. This tends to happen when they see others having success with other trees. They start to think, "What am I doing, trying to grow a Chinese bamboo tree? If I had planted a lime tree, I'd have a few limes by now." These are the people who return to their old jobs and their old ways. They walk away from their dream in exchange for a "sure thing."

Sadly, what they fail to realise is that pursuing your dream is a sure thing if you just don't give up. So long as you keep watering and fertilising your dream, it will come to fruition, just like the Chinese bamboo tree. It may take weeks. It may take months. It will most likely take years, but eventually, the roots will take hold and your Chinese bamboo tree will grow. And when it does, it will grow in remarkable ways.

The grass is greener where you water it!

We've seen this happen so many times. R.U. Darby had to water his Chinese bamboo tree through giving up on gold before he finally succeeded with the insurance business. Another great bamboo grower was Michael Jordan, getting cut from his team to then go and spend a year immersing himself in the game of basketball, practising every day before he cracked it, which led him to play, grow, and succeed in the NBA.

Well, you have a Chinese bamboo tree inside of you just waiting to break through. So keep watering and believing and you too will grow to the heights you dream of.

My question to you: what will you start doing differently because of this little, yet powerful story of the Chinese bamboo tree?

4. Harvesting Rewards (Excavate)

The greatest achievement is the feeling you get once you solve a problem, achieve a goal, book the dream holiday. Harvesting any reward is an amazing feat but how long do you give yourself to enjoy the reward before setting the next challenge or goal? I believe this is why the journey becomes so important with feeling fulfilled. Doesn't matter how tough the journey will be because the first time on any adventure, the journey is sure to be tough, and you must enjoy it. Celebrate every small win. Celebrate every small step you take. The more enjoyable the journey the longer the positive feelings will stay around. Play your own game. Your dreams are not a race, nor is it a destination. It's a feeling you have once you're there. If the journey is as important as the dream then why not celebrate those feelings now when you're on the path ? If you are taking small steps then why not have a piece of happiness now? Isn't the dream already a reality if you take the action and enjoy the process just like the bamboo tree?

5. Circle of Five

Once you have recognised opportunity, made the decision to water the opportunity as that's where it will become greener. You have committed to the journey, you are enjoying lots of positive emotions; the last piece of the puzzle, I believe, is creating your circle of five.

Motivational speaker Jim Rohn famously quotes: "You are the average of the five people you spend the most time with." The bottom line is, the people around you matter. You need people—whether it's co-founders, mentors, family, or friends—who will challenge you and make you better, thereby raising your average or helping you maintain a high one.

I love this quote for one reason and that is I can influence my wellbeing by spending time with the right people.

Create your circle of five! Now is it currently happening by default or is it by design?

I believe this should be a mix of loved ones, friends, mentors, and mentees to get the right balance to influence you in a way that you can keep moving to where you want to go while enjoying the process.

Depending on where you are or what you want with your journey will depend on whom you need to be spending more time with.

My current circle of five is my partner, as that's my emotional support, three people I'm currently mentoring, and then the last is my personal mentor. This doesn't mean I don't spend time with friends, it's that at this moment this is where I'm investing my time to achieve the outcome I desire.

Next month it may be my partner, two close friends, one person I'm coaching, and someone that's mentoring me. I believe the most important people are the ones that are supportive, care, are honest with you, and help you on your journey. Sometimes the biggest mistake we make when we look at our circle of five is that we have no one on there who is coaching us on how to achieve our dreams. Sometimes we look at our circle of five and it's people we don't care about and we are wondering why we feel uninspired.

Write down your current circle of five and how they are adding value to your life. It's not about cutting people out of your life, it's about spending more time with people that will help you move forward. Always have a mentor, someone you love, family or friends, and lastly someone to whom you can add value to their life.

So if your vibe attracts your tribe then who you spend the most time with will influence this.

CHAPTER 3

The Importance of Sales

1. Everything You Do in Life, Sales Will Be Needed

Even as a father I need to sell to my daughter on why she needs to wear warm clothes in winter.

Taking my daughter Ava to the shops or even choosing an outfit to wear can sometimes be the ultimate battle; Ava tests every bit of my sales skills I have developed over the years: my resilience, persistence, and not getting frustrated. I have had to insert a huge amount of mental energy to master and outwit a clever, stubborn five-year-old girl turning 15.

I would say that my daughter is a fashionista; she loves fashion, accessories, colour, Ava is a very creative girl. On a cold, rainy winter's day Ava will choose a summer outfit as if going to the beach which would consist of a lovely bright pink tutu, black boots, purple nail polish, and a bright yellow t-shirt. Now I'm not sold on the combination, but Ava is. Mismatched clothing I can handle as Ava is super excited, we want Ava to express herself with the choice of colour and style, but it's seven degrees outside, I'm completely wrapped from head to toe, its freezing inside, let alone outside. I know within five minutes of leaving the house Ava will say "I'm cold" which I attempt to warn Ava of multiple times, Ava giving me a blank look with no emotion. I can just imagine her thoughts: *Dad, what are you talking about, I know what I want,* so I can see the outcome I need, it's just how to get there.

I have faced the same situation multiple times before, not only with Ava, but negotiating a massive contract or persuading a customer/client to use our services, or convincing my girlfriend to watch an action movie over a romantic comedy. All situations are as challenging as each other, with your loved ones sometimes more so. Dealing with Ava I have learnt the hard way: sometimes after arguing for hours on choice of clothing, neither of us back down. Okay, so the trick is preparing an outfit needs to start the night before, with talking about what we are doing the next day and painting a picture of the outcome, then subtly suggesting the best outfit to wear regarding the climate conditions, expressing how amazing Ava will look in her new-found choice, and negotiating with the accessories. The negotiation must start the night before giving Ava the choice of clothing types. Preparing a sales presentation is very similar to dealing with children, partners, family, friends, customers, clients, and colleagues. If you choose not to have a sales presentation and to follow a no-negotiation policy, running everything like a dictatorship just telling someone what to do, forcing someone to buy, can end in resentment, hesitation, remorse, tears, anger, and with yourself getting left frustrated. Even if the outcome is achieved, how will everyone feel, and are you empowering people, getting them excited, or just making the decision? No one wants to be told what to do; everyone wants an element of choice. The art of communication is prevalent in all day-to-day activities, even the smallest of tasks will require salesmanship.

I believe sales is the most important life skill to learn. Communication is the key in delivering your unique message to all humans on the planet. If you are to have success in getting the girl of your dreams, getting employed at your first job, getting your foot in the door with your dream career, signing your first client, starting your own business, raising children, building long-lasting friendships, the art of salesmanship is key. Communication is the source of all growth. We are all in sales, like it or not. As soon as you make peace with this only then will you start not only loving the process but living a life on your terms.

2. Every Business Globally Is Selling Something: An Idea, Product, Service, Or Yourself/Themselves

People spend so much time making their products, ideas, or services great. How much time do you invest in developing sales skills in yourself to be GREAT! To guarantee every chance your idea, product, service will flourish. The secret has always been getting others to buy into you before what you can offer anyone.

Ask for that pay rise you deserve, get that promotion you have always wanted, work for that company you have always dreamed of, approach the girl you always loved. In most cases if done in the right way the worst thing that will ever happen is getting a no. Yes, getting the no hurts, not only our ego but our hearts, but why wait to see what will happen, at least you now have an opportunity to move on without wasting valuable time. Sometimes in these situations is when opportunity presents itself. In these times, this is when people are open to you with what you need to improve on or if you have a chance to be successful. The most important part is it gives you an opportunity to go back to the drawing board on how to improve the sales presentation or to move on to the next potential candidate which may be more suited.

3. My Love For Sales

I remember one of the first sales opportunities I had, it was a fun run that was organised through the school. I was 10 years old. Now I'm not sure why it was called a fun run as you had to run laps on the oval and that for sure wasn't very fun, especially puffing your way to victory. It was a great idea in terms of raising money for a charitable cause. The idea of the fun run was to get sponsors to give you donations to run; if you completed the run the money would go to charity. Based on the level of income raised you would get different prizes. The more money you raised the better the prize. The prize I had my eye on was glow-in-the-dark stars.

This is when I became excited and the vison of having an amazing prize was enough motivation for me. After school, I would knock on every door; rejection after rejection, I would still canvass my neighbourhood until well after dark, the stars in the night sky that would come out was fuel for me to get a few more donations. I asked all family members for donations, even the same ones multiple times, I begged my mum to get sponsors for me at her work. With this determination and after lots of rejection, the yes's started to come. Every yes gave me a feeling of accomplishment, the belief I needed to find the next yes. I raised hundreds of dollars and chose my prize which was of course the glow-in-the-dark stars which I stuck up and covered the whole celling in my bedroom; my room looked like the Milky Way and every time I went to bed it was a reminder of what I achieved. Little did I know this is where my love of sales started. How taking action allows you to reach your dreams if the desire is there. How if I focused on an outcome a lot can be achieved; the understanding of the importance of sales and taking action started for me at a young age and this was my first taste of manifestation of my dreams/vision or goal.

4. The Stigma of Sales

To many people, the word *selling* implies manipulating, pressuring, aggressive tactics, and forcing people to buy. The reason why is for years individuals were trying to fit a square peg in a round hole, selling a solution to a problem they didn't have or understand. If certain people took the time to understand their problem then the right solution would be found. Greedy individuals damage the reputation for the sales industry by selling customers what they don't need. I'm sure it's only a small percentage that do, so how can we let a small percentage affect our views on the largest industry on the planet? My perception before getting involved in opening my business was every sales person was desperate, it was my lack of education that was to blame and I often confused enthusiasm for desperation. It's a shame we have this negative connection with sales. Having a good understanding of business now, I know how important reputation and transparency is and how hard people work to protect their brands.

Saying you don't like sales is selling someone on the idea of not liking sales, so you are selling. We all have opinions we like to be heard to share our positive or negative views, experiences with people either face to face, or online. Salesmanship is the idea of getting buy-in from the people we are communicating with.

In any working environment, without the skill of sales you won't succeed. Like in everyday life sales are important to use in the workplace, it doesn't matter what industry you're in, or what aspect of your life you want to improve. This is the one thing all successful people know how to do well.

If you think of *selling* as explaining the logic and benefits of a decision, then everyone, business owner or not, needs sales skills. To convince others that an idea makes sense, to show bosses or investors how a project or business will generate a return, to help employees understand the benefits of a new process, or convince your daughter to wear warm clothes in winter.

People struggle with sales because of the perception and the fear of rejection. People spend their entire lives avoiding the word **no**; it is as inevitable to get one as it is getting a **yes**. The law of averages suggests that upon receiving a no, a yes is inevitable, it's only a matter of time. A yes will happen as long as you don't give up before the yes comes.

In essence, sales skills are communication skills. Communication skills are critical in any life situation, business, or career and you'll learn more about communication by working in sales than you will anywhere else. If you have ever convinced a friend to watch a movie you wanted to watch, or a partner to go to a restaurant you wanted, convinced a police officer to let you off a fine, this is the foundation to salesmanship, the art form of sales.

5. Daniel Tonkin's Top 24 Tips and Benefits on Selling

I believe with the tips below and with a solid understanding of the benefits on offer, you can start taking action to influence your dreams. Sales and communication is a great foundation to build from. The greater the foundation the stronger the building (dream).

1. Mentality, mentality, mentality

   I believe all sales/dreams are make or break before you have even showered or left the house in the morning. Building on your belief systems is the most important aspect of achieving any endeavour. If you wake up and feel disempowered it will most likely follow you throughout the day. Look for ways of educating yourself, to influence the way you think. Read a book, phone a mentor, ask questions. Become a google master, its so easy to Research and study, just type into google "How to sell ..." "or "How to stay motivated?" you will get access to hundreds of articles, clips and information. Education will help master your thoughts or put you in a position to believe you will achieve. You will need to absolutely 100% believe in your product (yourself) to succeed.

2. Don't be afraid to ask

   If it's for a pay rise? Another opportunity? A promotion? More money from a customer? Money from an investor?

   Keep asking until a no is presented; you will never know how much someone is willing to spend/ invest until they say no. If you don't ask you will not receive. No means I'm not convinced at the current time so revisit later. Those who ask shall receive.

3. Teach people how to sell!

   This can Influence your life in a big way. The best way to retain information is to teach the information, the main point is it helps you become consciously aware. As once you have been doing sales for a while you go into auto pilot. Letting yourself be unconsciously aware makes it easy to forget what works. The best reminder of a working strategy is teaching someone else as you need to become consciously aware to master coaching.

4. Have a structure you follow
   Doesn't mean you need to be a robot but it gives you confidence and allows you to find consistency and then also pass on the information.

5. Have fun!
   Don't take yourself too seriously! You can have fun and still take work seriously. The first interaction is always important so ice breaker first. Nothing sells better than entertainment. Entertain them before selling. Enjoy every interaction and it will feel you never worked a day in your life. You got to love the rush. The pleasure of the transaction. The winning feeling.

6. Use analogies to paint a picture for your customers
   This creates not only a more colourful dialogue it creates transparency. Facts tell, stories sell.

7. Character building
   Sales is going to teach you valuable life lessons like how to deal with rejection as it will happen to everyone at some point in life, bouncing back from the downturns, communicating effectively, building your confidence; it's why so many top CEOs, business owners, and billionaires come from a sales background. The rejection you deal with in sales day to day gets you ready for the shit that happens with life. It builds on your mental toughness. Helps you get to the rainbows.

8. Not everyone can do sales
   I hear statements like this: often to be good at sales you must have the gift of the gab, or this person is great as they could sell ice to an Eskimo. Anyone who believes this is fooling themselves, it's a massive myth and an absolute load of shit. Get this out of your head ASAP. You have two ears and one mouth, if you listen more

than you talk you are already ahead of individuals that talk too much.

9. Body language (become a master)
   Albert Mehrabian did a study into understanding feelings and one's attitude. How understanding emotions will help influence sales. He broke it down into three areas to focus on, that helps someone become a buying customer.
   Words (the literal meaning) account for 7% of the overall message
   Tone of voice accounts for 38% of the overall message
   Body language accounts for 55% of the overall message
   To become a master communicator, you must understand how to influence your body language accordingly. The areas you can improve such behaviours include facial expressions, body posture, gestures, eye movement, touch, and the use of space.

10. Never give up (three feet away from gold)
    Understanding Darby's misfortune will help you in your journey. When I lost $100K in 10 weeks, my dream was over. I stayed on the path even though I wanted to give up. When I finally reached the gold I was looking for I thought I can't believe I was so close to giving up. My definition of success is doing the things you said you were going to do even when the feeling is gone. It's easy to be motivated when all is well, what will get you through the tough times?

11. You will get free shit all the time
    If it's an upgrade on a plane, free wine at a restaurant, or better seats at a sporting venue, when you have mastered the art of communication, you will have a nice vibe about you that people will draw to. The key is just be a nice person to everyone, stay humble. My friends often say to me, do you know that person? Why did we get an upgrade or free wine? My answer is simple: be nice and stay humble.

12. What is your brand?
    You are always building on your reputation. Is it ethical, reliant, focused: what does your brand stand for? Your name will be the foundation of the brand you build and is it a reputable one?
    You need to do everything compliantly, lawfully if you want your dreams to last long term. Don't make the mistake in creating short cuts. The only short cut is learning from experience.

13. Communication will improve and open more opportunities.
    When your communication skills are enhanced people will take notice and new opportunities will present themselves. You still need to say "yes."
    Ask the right questions, don't "pitch" your potential customers. Having a two-way communication platform is commonly known as a conversation and that is my focus every time. People buy off people. We love to interact with others, hence why face-to-face sales will always be around.

14. Know your numbers; what are your KPIs?
    If you don't have key performance indictors or a way to measure results how do you coach yourself or how can others coach you to improve?
    To work your law of averages, change it from an emotional game to a mathematical game, to do that you need your numbers.

15. Be honest and sincere, no bullshit or deceit.
    When trust is formed it's the difference between being around for a long time versus a short time.

16. Sometimes people are dickheads, don't let it affect your dreams.
    We all enjoy roller coasters for the instant thrill. Sales/life can have many highs and lows so strap in and enjoy the ride. Don't take rejection personally, especially from rude people. Understand you can only influence not control people. Always try to leave someone feeling great no matter the situation as you never know what can happen down the track or whats going on in that persons life.

17. Be patient
    Give yourself time to get good. Just like everything, the more you spend time on it, the better you get.

18. You need a strong work ethic
    Warren Buffet famously quotes: "The harder you work the luckier you get."
    I love working hard as it allows me to take action and not get stuck in my own head, which often leads to overanalysing every situation. When I over analyse I often find myself sitting in procrastination. Work your arse off.

19. You'll learn to negotiate
    Every job involves negotiating, with customers, with vendors and suppliers, even with employees. Salespeople learn to listen, evaluate variables, identify key drivers, overcome objections, and find ways to reach agreement—without burning bridges.

20. You'll learn to close
    Asking for what you want is difficult for a lot of people. Closing a sale is part art, part science. Getting others to agree with you and follow your direction is also part art and part science. If you want to lead people, you must be able to close. Great salespeople know how to close. Great bosses do, too.

21. You'll learn persistence
    Salespeople hear the word *no* all the time. Over time you'll start to see *no* as a challenge, not a rejection. And you'll figure out what to do next.

22. You'll learn self-discipline
    When you work for a big company, you can sometimes sleepwalk your way through a day and still get paid. When you work on commission, your credo is, "If it is to be, it's up to me." Working in sales is a fantastic way to permanently connect the mental dots between performance and reward.

The Importance of Sales

23. You'll gain self-confidence

    Working in sales is the perfect cure for shyness. You'll learn to step forward with confidence, especially under duress or in a crisis.

    Still not convinced? Think of it this way: The more intimidating or scary a position in sales sounds, the more you need to take one. You'll gain confidence and self-assurance, and the skills you gain will serve you well for the rest of your business—and personal—life.

    So if you're a would-be entrepreneur, set aside your business plan and work in sales for a year or two. If you're a struggling entrepreneur, take a part-time sales job. Part of the reason you're struggling is probably because of poor sales skills.

    Successful business owners spend the majority of their time "selling."

    Go learn how to sell.

    It's the best investment you will ever make.

24. Love what sales can give you

    Fundraising for the fun run taught me one crucial lesson. If I master sales I can create a life and lifestyle of choice. The fun run taught me to work for myself and how to influence your emotions when you have the desire. Excitement is easy to call on when you're on a mission and can feel, taste, and see the rewards come to fruition. Yes, there are setbacks but treat them like speed bumps in the road: they will slow you down (depending on what type of driver you are) but it won't stop you. You will be the only reason the reward becomes out of reach. The mentality I use today inside my business is the same one I had as a 10-year-old, only difference is the rewards have changed. I no longer want glow-in-the-dark stars on my ceiling—funny that.

When I first stumbled upon the law of attraction—which is the belief that positive thoughts are **magnets** for positive **life** experiences and negative thoughts are magnets for negative life experiences. *Based on the* *law of attraction, if you have a specific* **desire** *and* **focus** *joyfully on that desire, it* **will** *be fulfilled*—the idea made sense to me and I thought *yes, I am a big dreamer, I think positive, so a lot of my dreams will turn into reality.* Unfortunately, without taking action a lot of the outcomes will eventually turn into an idea that will be long forgotten. The art form, mindset, and determination of a sales person is a great building block of any outcome. It teaches you how it influences your way of thinking and not to let the negative aspects affect you day to day. I truly believe salesmanship is the missing ingredient to make any dreams become a reality. Sales will build on your emotional intelligence with that you can influence whole communities, markets and be the leader you deserve to be.

With everything I have shared my final thoughts.

What are you doing today to master the sales process and build on your communication skills?

CHAPTER 4

Supressing Emotions Got Me Nowhere

1. Love and Trust

After choosing supressing emotions got me nowhere as the title of the chapter, I was instantly overwhelmed with a wide range of emotions and thoughts. I began to word vomit into my laptop, banging on the keyboard, expressing a lot of feelings that I wanted to share as I can imagine others would be experiencing the same emotional rollercoaster I once did.

Did I knowingly suppress emotions? When asked about events that happened in my life that seemed major I was always nonchalant about the event. Was this an indication of me suppressing my emotions? I'm a male; we don't talk about emotions to anyone, we don't get down—that is weak.

Fear had stopped me in my tracks many times, so I wanted to learn what fear was. After hours of reading and research it seemed most people were affected globally by the same three universal fears which are: Will I belong? Will I be found out? Will I be loved? The realisation I had was profound. It made so much sense why public speaking was the number one fear on the planet today. The three fears holding us back: Will I belong? Will I be accepted by my peers? I'm afraid I will be judged if I don't say the right thing. Will I be found out? I'm not good enough, I don't deserve. Will I be loved? Will people like me, am I loveable? To those three fears I say, fuck them. Cursing at the fears probably doesn't help but if you have an understanding of the fears you now have an opportunity to work on them.

These three fears were stopping me from accessing love and trust. I found it was easier to fight them unresourcefully as I didn't need to face them; I could cover the issues with a Band-Aid fix and create a new story. With trust, I would lie about events that seemed uneventful to others but would make my story sound more appealing to me, no one would know the real me, so if I was rejected I was protected. With love, I didn't really believe in relationships, marriages, families as they all seem to eventually break down. Womanising seemed like a viable option to fill the gap, so if I did get involved in any new relationship I was always thinking should I end it now, or how to create a distance between us, sabotaging the relationship early on as it wouldn't work out anyway. If I was to be resourceful with those two emotions I would've confronted the overriding challenges and maybe I could've felt freedom in my mind earlier.

What drives our ego is the six core needs which are significance, love/connection, uncertainty, certainty, contribution, and growth. Core needs are said to dictate every action, thought, and feeling we experience.

Feelings that may be experienced when you're not meeting your ego's needs are overwhelm, disconnection, unhappiness, depression, anxiety, boredom, and feelings of frustration which interesting enough were the exact feelings I was going through.

When we are fulfilling our needs resourcefully we can feel contentment, self-drive, love, and feelings of fulfilment which I now feel day to day once I took action.

A major event or events which happen throughout our life can often play havoc on our mind. Sometimes you don't remember the event that had an impact on your life, sometimes you can trace back to the exact event that triggered the actions you act on to protect your ego. As a six-year-old, not much older than my daughter, I would go on adventures all around our neighbourhood. Our neighbourhood was surrounded by bush so it was the perfect place to explore. Our street was full of kids around my age. Each day all the kids would get together, we would go on adventures to see areas we hadn't yet encountered; we were surrounded by bushland so a lot of places were left uncharted, each adventure we would go deeper into the bush. On one day, not too different to any other day, I set out with two other children deep into the bush to find a new cubby house to play in. As I'm writing a great sadness fills my heart as it beats a million miles a second.

One of the children was murdered by a stranger.

From that day, I didn't let anyone in and this is when the lies started. I'm very fortunate to have survived. As a father now, I can imagine the pain the parents/family members would've and still are going through. My heart and condolences still goes out to them. It was an event that had a massive impact on my life but it wouldn't reveal itself until I was in my early 20s. I made that event mean I couldn't trust anyone and for years I would guard myself, never fully letting people in to the real Daniel. I would lie about my past to make my story more compelling to me, never fully opening up to anyone and only telling parts of my story.

In my early twenties, anxiety started to consume me, the symptoms I started to experience were similar to PTSD which is post-traumatic stress syndrome. It was hard for me to get through the days. I would keep myself very busy to hide the pain. Working crazy long hours, consuming alcohol, dealing with my problems unresourcefully. Growing up I didn't reflect on the major event, in the back of my subconscious it was brewing. I realised I had a mental illness that needed to be addressed so I went and sought professional help. By this time, I was 28 and already living with fear for 22 years.

How was I going to overcome one of my ultimate hurdles?

The world is fucked and full of monsters but the world is also amazing and full of love. I had to take the first step, it was either towards blame, denial or to truth and freedom. Don't ever think you're too tough, that nothing fazes you. That in itself is a warning sign. I got offered plenty of support over the years but I refused it. I was going to be fine as men are supposed to be fine. Everyone has their own issues to deal with, don't let it consume you. You deserve to live a life without fear. Sometimes you don't know you have a problem or your mind hides it from you to protect yourself. I'm telling you this because as men we can open up and be honest. When I finally got help it was like a breath of fresh air, the world seemed so different, more refreshing. I could finally be the man I always wanted to be, which was me. I was happy to just be me. Once I started taking action on my demons everything around me changed, not straight away but slowly and the more action I took the better I felt. My only advice is go find a mentor, someone that can listen to you and help come up with solutions together. Free yourself from your mind. We all have issues; there isn't an individual anywhere that isn't going through something, so stop punishing yourself.

I'm thankful I'm alive and I want you to be thankful!

What are you thankful for in your life?

Is there anything you are facing you would want support with?

Will you promise yourself you will start working on YOU, as you deserve it?

2. Emotional Intelligence vs Intelligence Quotient or EI vs IQ

I believe a major part of me overcoming my demons was understanding my emotions and gathering intelligence around why I do things, why I make decisions the way I do, and what drives me. Most decisions humans make are emotional ones, so if I was to be emotional with my decision process I wanted to own that decision and if emotions were going to control my life then at least influence the emotions you want in your life. IQ was always seen in the early days as what was needed to have success in your life. Getting a university degree was of high importance. University doesn't guarantee your success and I believe working on your emotional wellbeing and understanding other people's emotions will give you a higher chance of success. Emotional intelligence is the capability of individuals to recognise their own and other people's emotions. People with a high EI have greater mental health, job performance, and are happier. Understanding emotions was a key factor for me with understanding myself and then I had the ability to help others create success.

3. Marriage, Why?

As a young kid growing up looking at everyone in my family, not one person was still married to their first wife/husband. My grandparents, my parents, and all my aunties and uncles were divorced or remarried. Which meant the family was also broken up. Now for me I made that mean that love was never long lasting. I again protected my ego, I hid my heart and emotions so it couldn't ever be broken or hurt. The problem is I was hiding from love and not allowing love to come to me because I was fearful of losing it. I had this thought about marriage, what's the point if it isn't going to last. "It is better to have loved and lost than never to have loved before." I heard the quote so many times I thought "it was cheesy." It did have its truths, without love joy disappears, life becomes mundane. If I gave a fuck about anything it would be love and that's worth fighting for. Love for my family, friends, business, food, and all things I'm passionate about. Love makes everything taste better, look better, and feel better. Stop protecting yourself and open up. Yes, you will get hurt but you will be stronger each time. Decide what you think is worth fighting for.

What are your current beliefs about love?

How do you see yourself having more love in your life?

4. How to Overcome Overwhelm

Overwhelm is a dream killer, it has taken down a lot of people's futures. Overwhelm is a killer of action and a breeder of procrastination. Overwhelm usually comes once a week, it takes over my life and I can't do anything. I get pretty much zero done on the days of overwhelm. There is no motivation to do anything when there's **everything** to do. I've laid in bed for hours thinking about the amazing number of things that needed to get done before finally sleeping through exhaustion. Then when I get out of bed in the morning before leaving for work I get on my computer or electronic notepad and look at what needs to be done and I'm overloaded with tasks that the only thing I could do is go look at Facebook to distract myself. Then the day is finished just as quick as it starts, it's time for dinner, then sleep, but I can't sleep because I'm thinking of everything I didn't do today.

What a cycle!

Overwhelm comes from us putting too many projects on our plate and losing track of them, or from taking no action then suddenly there is a build-up of tasks, or my personal favourite, having everything that's happening in your life in your head and trying to make sense of it all. People live in a constant state of overwhelm as so many of us are so busy trying to get things done so many things are left out. A major part of me over coming overwhelm and influencing my emotions was doing a weekly brain dump. I would find a quiet place once a week and write down every thought that would exist in my brain. I would create a massive list of random thoughts, things I needed to do, people I needed to talk to, weird dreams. Now step one is getting everything out of your head and down on paper or electronic device. I always feel instant clarity once this is done, normally taking me an hour to do. The challenge I had initially was I would do the brain dump and feel great then after two days the overwhelm would come back and the cycle then continues. The secret is you must take action on your brain dump. I would create a list and number the brain dump from one to wherever the list finished; I would then create my own key.

- ■ I need to take action today.
- ● I need to take action by the end of the week.
- ▲ I need to take action by the end of the month.
- ○ I need to take action this quarter.
- △ I need to take action this year.
- □ I need to take action at some point in my life.
- ◆ No need to take action.

I would put a symbol next to each thought, I would then write a time, day I would take action on that thought. The reason I never took action as some thoughts were I want to buy a house, the thought seemed so big that I would dismiss it. Instead of dismissing the thought I put a * next to the thought which stands for take action this week. I would then write what small action I would take so it would be to set up a bank account that said home loan and started transferring $20 a week into the account. Then have a date and time I would complete the activity so I can manage my time effectively. It's not about doing everything on the list today, it's about taking even the smallest of actions so you can free your mind of clutter and start feeling like you're moving forward. I would revisit the list weekly, then add thoughts on and take thoughts off. The brain dump is the ultimate to-do list. I will give you an example on how to use the symbols.

Brain dump

1. Buy a house. ● I will set up a bank account and transfer $20 a week into a new account labelled home. I will do it Friday night at seven p.m.
2. Buy a present for girlfriend. ▲ I will Google ideas Friday at 7.30 p.m. after I set up bank account but I don't need to buy till end of the month.
3. Finish strategy plan for quarter four. ○ I will revisit.
4. Go to the gym. ● I will go Monday, Wed, Thursday after work at six p.m.
5. Weird dream about black spiders chasing me. ◆ no need for action just a weird dream.

6. Need to increase sales in perfume product line. ● I will look at results and have a strategy meeting with senior staff Wednesday at nine a.m.
7. What am I going to do when I retire? ^ revisit later.

I found once I started looking at my brain dump weekly, I had times, days also locked in. I found I had so much time to do things and it was so easy to organise myself. The habit allows me to run multiple businesses and live a life I want. No more overwhelm or if it does hit me it leaves me very quickly once I look at the list and see I have a plan to address it.

5. Be Yourself

Being selfish will allow you to be selfless. It doesn't mean you do not care about others, it's the opposite. If you want to have an impact on people's lives then by living a life others would love to emulate that will have the impact you desire. Make sure you **do you!** Everyone will have an idea on the life you should lead. A lot of emotional stress is caused from people doing things that others want them to do. I know because I also did this. Only you know what you want so stay true to yourself.

Love and trust were emotional mountains larger than Everest that I overcame. Suppressing my emotions only held me back and once I faced them I was finally free from my mind. Understanding fear and how your ego plays out will be pivotal with your own emotional wellbeing. We aren't always responsible for the terrible tragedies that happen in our lives but we are responsible for how we deal with them and the impact they leave on us and how they impact the people in our lives.

What's holding you back?

Are you ready to face them head on?

CHAPTER 5

What Is Your Dream?

1. Are You Building Your Dream or Someone Else's?

A quote that has always stuck in my head is "Build your dream or someone will hire you to build theirs."

I understand the quote but what is the answer to the overriding question? What is my dream? The answer isn't as straightforward as be your own boss. The concept I understand: being an entrepreneur it's easier to build your dream as every day is a reminder you work for yourself, you have an element of freedom and your actions are hopefully building towards a future. In other environments, it can be challenging as maybe you can't connect your dreams with what you are doing day to day which causes you to feel uninspired, unmotivated and confused with no purpose.

The message underlying in the quote is if you take ownership of your situation, choose a vehicle to take you towards your dream, no matter what the vehicle is, that is essential to living a life of purpose or "building your dream vs someone elses" Even a Buddhist monk has a purpose to get to enlightenment.

What are you going to choose to give a fuck about?

2. Voices Inside My Head

There is so much noise on the planet today it's hard to know what your inner voice is saying to you.

Three things that are always in contest in your mind are your inner voice, thoughts, and the ego. Which one is real?

You will notice when you are deep in thought you can narrate them. I call that your inner voice; it's very different than your thoughts and can influence your thinking and dictate your actions. The ego, on the other hand, sways influence on your inner voice and thoughts; the ego always wants more and if it's not getting it resourcefully, it will get it un-resourcefully. Be careful of the ego as it has an insatiable hunger for more! More good and more bad. Just more.

These three play out in your mind constantly, it's like an internal power struggle—good versus evil. They all never seem to win. With all this craziness going on inside our head I understand why so many of us don't think about what our dreams are.

I have asked one question over a thousand times to colleagues over the years. What is your dream?

Apart from the initial pause and stumble the majority of people I ask replied with either I don't know, maybe it's to be happy, or get my dream job, start my own family, support my family, financial freedom, house by the sea, or buy a Ferrari. It seems not much thought had gone into the answer which is perfectly fine.

What point do you make the decision?

Now you have dreams you need to know what emotions would the dreams give you once they were achieved?

If your dream is getting a multi-million dollar house on the beach remember that's the end destination. I focus more on the emotions I want to experience and emulate that. What emotions do you feel spending time close to water? Is it freedom, or calm? If you love the feeling of going to the beach, seeing or being around water then make sure you experience water more often. If you can connect with the emotions early on, two things will happen. One - you will realise you have everything you want, so you don't need the beach house. Or two, you will realise that you really want the beach house, and now you must have it.

No point having a dream to buy a multimillion beach house if you don't know what it looks like, how much it costs, if you haven't checked out multiple locations, or been to home openings so you understand price and then never saving towards it; you will never achieve your dream and will most likely be unsatisfied with your life if that's all you gave a fuck about.

Questions to ask yourself:
1. Are you prepared to dedicate a large part of your life making the dream a reality?
2. Do you talk about your dream? Is it written down, pictures of the outcome surrounding you?
3. Do you actually care if it happens or not?

If the answer is no, get a dream quick, choose what problems you want to solve, and then act. An overriding dream or future big picture is essential so you know where you're going and what you give a fuck about. For me a dream is always long-term aspirations or future you.

3. If You Don't Have a Bucket List, You Probably Don't Have a Crystal-Clear Vision

Isn't the dream to live life and have peace, euphoria, ecstasy, love, and all emotions that let you submit to past and future. Totally live in the now.

Once you have a dream the bucket list gives you short bursts of enthusiasm. It's great for short-term focuses and reminds you of the dream to come. It's easy to forget the dream when life is happening. I need reminders, to have fun, to have love in my life, and bucket lists give me short-term drive to create the emotions I want to emulate long term.

Ticking off 70/80% of your bucket list each year is imperative in making your dream a reality. It gives you longevity in the tough years and maximises the good years.

Bucket lists are one of the most simplistic ways to get yourself feeling good day to day and giving yourself things to be excited about. I love doing a new bucket list each year as it's easier to be focused on it. Of course, I have an overriding dream I'm slowly working towards. Dreams are often so far in the future that if we don't emulate the feelings of the future dream it can often be left aside. For example, if I wanted to fly or become a pilot and I was working full time maybe in my one-year bucket list it could be take one flying lesson this year. That would engage the feeling of my future dream and help build momentum towards my new future. As babies, we are very good at dictating our wants! We cry when we are hungry, sick, need to change our pooey nappies (uncomfortable), or we just want love and attention. Bucket lists give us the same emotions but allow us to influence our emotions over a longer period of time.

My bucket lists range from free activities, normal-priced experiences, to expensive travel trips.

The key is keeping you and whoever is in your life engaged.

Some free examples on my 2017 bucket list were to read six books, pretty basic as I was spending a lot of time writing my own book. I had spending time at five beaches I hadn't been to before, anything that is free and I love doing, I add it to my bucket list so I can make myself accountable. A medium price example would be I love food so we choose 12 restaurants we want to go to, then booking one in every month (my fiancé, wife-to-be, does this for us); the more people involved in the bucket list the better. An expensive example in 2017 was going to Canada, USA for a month. If your bucket list is completed in January, make sure you have a plan to take action, then the feeling you will have throughout the year is love, joy, and excitement as there is always something to look forward to. This is the best way to get the most out of yourself, also a great starting point to live life on your terms.

I like to have around 20-30 points on my bucket list so around two to tick off each month.

I base my bucket list on what I love, what makes me feel free, what's great for my health, what gives me excitement, what I can learn, how I can challenge myself, and what I want to buy.

You have a dream!

Get your yearly bucket list done today!

4. Where Is Your Nav Man, Google Maps, or Whatever Navigational Device You Use Leading You To?

My very first year in Sydney moving from Perth I got beeped at and abused on the road every day. I was thinking, what is wrong with the Sydney drivers, assuming they were just impatient and all a bunch of wankers. I love driving, I always have, but Sydney was testing my love for driving, then after a year in Sydney the abuse and beeping stopped. When visiting Perth on holiday I see the problem: every car goes the same speed on every road, the overtaking lanes are non-existent, so if you want to overtake, well, good luck. In Perth when we are merging we decide to slow down, often stopping, causing massive traffic congestion; when the traffic light turns green we like to wait until orange to go and if someone has been pulled up by a cop, well, we all like to stop and look. This may sound like an overreaction and if you're from Perth you may be in denial like I was. I then realised if you have ever driven in Perth or know anyone that has you would know we are just shit drivers in general and it's not our fault, we don't know any better it's the culture.

This leads me into my love of using navigation while driving, I use navigation at every opportunity, even to the shops which I've been to hundreds of times I would be like "Babe, can we use the nav man or Google maps?" With a stern voice I get a "No" on most occasions. I love when the navigational device gives you an estimated time of arrival and you just want to beat it. If you shave off two minutes you feel like king of the road. If you go off track it just reroutes you so you always end up at the right destination, depending if you put the correct location, that is.

Once I have my dream, I now have my bucket list; all I need to do is enter the information into my nav man. My nav man is my plan and I need my plan to be as detailed as it could possibly be so if I go off track it can reroute me.

What I can say is I hated planning with a passion. I believe it's because I didn't understand the importance of it and I was a lazy shit. It's now a strength and something I spend a lot of time on; working on your life/business gives you great strategy and a plan implements it. You can't have one without the other. Don't just work in your life, work on your life.

What is in my plan?

I need to be able to break down my outcomes and make it specific (setting checkpoints), can I measure it (have key performance indicators), do I have specific time frames, is there action points around all my checklists so I don't procrastinate, if I went to an investor would they hand over cash to me based on my plan? Do I have someone or something keeping me accountable, does the whole plan make sense?

I feel planning is where most fault lies, everyone expects an amazing plan the first time sitting down and doing one. It took me hundreds of attempts to master it, lots of fucks-ups, hours of research, and a lot of advice to master the process. Mastering the process allows even large events in our life to be enjoyable. We are planning our wedding and even though we could hire someone to look after the details we are able to fully commit ourselves into organising it as we have all the right processes in place, We are able to have fun with the process with no stress.

Planning to me is just not missing out the details, allows you to cross the t's and dot the i's.

5. Stop Telling Yourself You Don't Know What You Want In Life

I completely get this statement. Deep down we all know what we want. We want to feel love, appreciated, and we all want to fit in. We all know what emotions we want to experience in our lives. The perfect job, the perfect home, the perfect book, the perfect partner isn't out there. It's what you make of every situation that will make it perfect for you. An Indian philosopher and spiritual teacher once said, "I don't mind what happens." He is content, as he understands all you have is the present, he believes there is no good or bad. Does this mean not to act to bring change in your life? On the contrary. It's making sure you have a dream you will stand by no matter the outcome; you follow a bucket list because those feelings are important and have a plan so your nav man can guide you. Will it work every time? No. The more you practice great habits you are giving yourself every chance to live life on your terms.

6. Don't Let Life Control You, Take Control of Your Life!

How business saved my life and how I can now live a life on my own terms.

It took years of me showing up to the office at seven a.m. and leaving at nine p.m. for me to realise I wasn't in control of my life! Sounds crazy, right? Who would want to put that much effort in anyway? Even if you have all the income in the world, when do you have time to spend it? Later? Tomorrow? I was creating something for my family, myself which meant I had a purpose. I felt I was on the right path. I was showing up every day, investing 14 hours a day into my business and thinking one day it will all change. Eventually I would have more time, eventually I would have more income, eventually I can do the things I want. We would all love to have more choices. I was building my business for the right reasons, so what was going wrong?

I was structuring my life in a way that I would never meet my purpose as I would burn out. I worked hard; isn't that enough?

How business saved my life? What a stupid title as it was killing me slowly. How many years can you sustain those hours, the stress on your body and mind? Then also maintaining purposeful relationships with loved ones. It was all a mess.

This is why I truly believe taking action allowed the business to be the vehicle that saved my life. Without business I doubt I ever would have found the answer to the greatest mysteries on earth! How to make yourself happy and live a life on your terms. Get your control back.

The great thing in business is you can make changes pretty quickly as you're the boss. I believe if I was an employee it would've taken me longer to realise, or possibly never at all. My previous career was a well-paid job, I was working hours similar to everyone else, you do a few holidays a year. That ain't too bad as everyone else is doing it, you get caught up in short term opportunities.

The dreams you had as a kid probably were unrealistic, did you settle on what you're doing now?

Whatever you do, don't risk change? What may happen? You may lose everything.

The older we get the more entitled we get; we should have nicer things, eat out more, spend more money, travel more. Entitlement stops us creating, risking, and keeps us settled/content on what we are doing. It doesn't get us dreaming.

Getting into business for me was like getting on the roller coaster of life. When I was employed it was like a merry-go-round.

I wanted the business roller coaster for adventure/creating my vision but also wanted the employed aspect of security knowing I will have money tomorrow.

What was the difference? It wasn't owning a business or being employed! It was taking ownership of my life and taking action on the things I wanted to be doing.

It all started when I decided on how I wanted to live my life; where did I want to dedicate my time, a goal of mine was always to give back to others. Help others solve their problems. I was creating more problems than solving. I knew I wanted to play life big so I would need to build something big.

So I started with a brain dump. It's not exactly what it reads like but at the same time it is. I wrote down everything that was going through my head! Dumped it onto paper. This was the turning point for me. I broke my massive dump into sections. Environment, so everything I needed to help me create a vision and understanding of what I'm about to do. Culture, creation, values, hours I wanted to work, beliefs, more holidays. Then my next section was systems and structures so what was needed for me to be able to do the things to create my environment. Implementation, so how was I going to take action and where to start. People, my team, family, mentors, or anyone that will have an impact. It's the ESIP model which worked and hang around, I will touch on this in Chapter 6.

I had been working so hard in my business I hadn't taken much time to work on the business. Instead of just building a business, shaping my life with what I want and then moulding the business around what I want to be doing.

We work to build a life we choose. Once I started living my life how I wanted it to be, by shaping my hours, times and actions around my passions, everything changed! I felt I had purpose, I felt great and I got my time back! I was in control of my life and life wasn't controlling me.

The brain dump is where you may need to start to clear the clutter and help you pull out your dream vision, get your bucket list (action points), create your plan.

7. Dreams Do Come True.

Knowingly or not the model I've shared is the backbone to every dream, vision, and experience I've ever had.

My very first dream as a 10-year-old to get the glow-in-the-dark stickers on the roof, from having negative $300 and turning that into $100,000 a year later, from winning new marketing company in 2009 then marketing company of the year in 2015, from now writing my book I get to share with the world, expanding my business into other countries, travel opportunities globally, living with water views, opening new businesses, spending time with my loved ones. Each part of my dream that I get to live is from following a simple strategy and taking action.

I don't have many skills. My gift, however, is taking action - which I want to share with others, so they can use my experience to empower themselves to live a life on their terms.

So, what is your dream?

When are you going to stop telling yourself you don't know your dream?

What are you going to put on your bucket list right now?

Are you going to keep listening to the voices in your head that say no?

Finally, are you going to build your dream or someone else's?

CHAPTER 6

The Daniel Tonkin Creation Strategy

1) Make/Create a Vision

As you all must be getting to know, I'm a massive advocate for stories. Most of us have heard variations of the lumber jack in the woods; this is one that I remember reading and copied.

> Once upon a time there were two men in a wood-chopping contest. They were tasked with chopping down as many trees in the forest as they could from sun-up to sundown. The winner would be rewarded with both fame and fortune.
>
> From morning till noon, both men steadily chopped and chopped. By noon they were neck and neck, but then one man took a break and stopped chopping. The other man saw this and thought to himself: *"While he breaks for lunch, he's given me a chance to get ahead of him and I will without a doubt win this contest!"*
>
> Soon after the man got back to work. As the day continued he chopped more trees than his hard-working (and hungry) competitor and by mid-afternoon he had taken a clear lead.
>
> When sundown came, the man who had taken the break at noon had chopped almost twice as many trees as the other man, who was drenched in sweat, hungry, and exhausted.

"*How did you beat me?*" he asked, puzzled. "*I outworked you and I didn't even take a break for lunch!*"

"Ah," said the other man, "*I did take a break, but it was during that break that I sharpened my axe.*"

Taking time out to sharpen your axe is worth many hours of hard work.

I loved this story as for the first part of my life I was the wood chopper that just worked hard; it didn't work for me, it was as if I lived my life on a treadmill. Sharpening my axe is the key to living the life I wanted. The right tools that have been sharpened, oiled or looked after in life will allow you to do more and get more with less energy. Tools are essential to any successful strategy and the most important tool is YOU!

Where to start? Like the lumber jack who sharpened his axe, start with the end in mind. With a clear outcome you are working towards taking breaks to sharpen your axe are important for longevity.

The purpose of this chapter is so you can walk away and create your own dream through using a proven strategy that works. This strategy I've used hundreds of times for various ideas and areas in my life.

The first tools I use are all based around creating a vision, having a vision, dream, outcome, goals; these are some words that do describe future aspirations. Without a vision I believe you travel through your life as a zombie; you only react when food is near.

After completing your brain dump (chapter 3, point 4, page 43-46) and getting everything out of your head, next is to complete a Mind map which is a tool I use to get a crystal-clear vision. It allows me to be creative and dream. This is where I start to formulate my thoughts and materialise them from my head to images.

1) Get a large sheet of paper preferably A3 or larger with as many colours of felt tip pens and pencils you can find.

2) The idea of mind mapping is visualising your future and how it will look like. Then drawing out the future on paper/or computer, wherever your skillset lies. If you want to draw, write, whatever is going to get your creative juices flowing. The map is a future image of your vision. I like to break down my future in a few areas to help with clarity. Family, business/work, income, investments, happiness, travel, health, recreation, adventure, possessions, making a difference to the world. You can add more areas to this list or remove some.

3) What time frames do I give? I like to do my vision for 20 years. It's effective with whatever time frame you give. The purpose is you need to get clarity, get everything inside your mind out so you can see what you want. You want to find your purpose, the things you will give a fuck about, fight for, and wake up for every day.

4) Once the creation phase is completed I want to make it real. Get real-life photos/pictures for each section. I want my vision to be super clear.

5) Now I have all the real photos I want to allocate time to sharpen my axe, to check in on my vision. Monthly, I suggest. I want to allocate checklists and action points with dates on when each will be achieved. I like to put costs next to the ones that will need financial investment so I can now measure my results.

6) This gives me a strong foundation to start to formulate a plan.

2) Plan

Vision is essential for getting your dreams and turning them into images and numbers but the plan is imperative for the creation phase. It's what allows the images/numbers to turn into reality. Paralysis by analysis is the killer of dreams in this phase. Overthinking leads to procrastination where I've witnessed many dreams endure a slow, quiet death.

Every thought, idea, vision, or a dream of mine once documented is then followed up with a **brainstorming session**. I write down everything I either know on the subject, need to know, and areas to consider. The most important part is getting everything out of your head again and down on paper, computer, or whiteboard as this will start to formulate what actions will be needed to turn it into a reality; this is different from creating a vision as there is substance and it's creating content into the context. The brainstorming session can be done on your own if you have experience or finding a mentor to help you structure the information is ideal.

The model I mentioned in Chapter 5 point 6, the **ESIP** model, allows you to follow a simple structure to help you create then implement an effective plan.

E- Environment

This is creating the reason **why** you do what you do, it is the foundation of what you will build your future aspirations on. Without the environment the building will become unstable. What makes up the environment is goals, vision, culture, purpose, attitude, values, mission statement, standards, and expectations. These are the pillars to your dream.

What are your goals? Are you currently working towards an outcome?

There are three types of goals needed first: Long-term goals which are five years plus the longer the goal the closer you will be to your ultimate purpose. Medium-term goals would be one year time frame; it's a great measurement for yourself as you reset and evaluate every year, I create my bucket lists yearly which gives me excitement and things to look forward to. It's easier to focus on as it can feel a lot closer. Short-term goals which I like having 90-day challenges or quarterly targets which gives me the action points I need to move me towards the yearly focus, and the most critical goal is the weekly goal. The weekly goal will determine how successful the long-term goal will be. I get bored very easily so having weekly checkpoints allows me to be accountable to my plan so I can work smarter, also I know the weekly target is connected to my big purpose so there is a reason behind what I'm doing versus just showing up each week to see what happens.

What to consider when creating a vision

Vision—mind mapping as a tool will allow you to sit down and create an ideal future. A vision is the ability to think about the future using imagination.

The **culture** (if you're in a team or family unit) is how a group of people will act and behave. Culture will allow a group of individuals to work together in unison with a shared view. In one of my businesses I created a family feel inside our business so everyone would support each other. In my family unit I create a loving, honest, and supportive culture.

Is there an overriding purpose? Why are you doing what you are doing? Does it connect to the long-term vision and give you a reason why you do what you do?

Attitudes—this is your mentality towards what you do, it's about how you and others choose to work/ live your life. We have all heard the phrase, have a can-do attitude. Attitude will set the right intentions when things aren't going to plan. Easy to be positive when things are working out well.

Values—your values are the things that you believe are important in the way you live and work. They (should) determine your priorities. Deep down, they're probably the measures you use to tell if your life is turning out the way you want it to. When the things that you do and the way you behave match your values, life is usually good—you're satisfied and content. But when these don't align with your personal values, that's when things feel ... wrong. This can be a real source of unhappiness. Therefore, making a conscious effort to identify your values is so important. Here are some examples of values we use inside my recruitment business.

Our Company Values

1. Fun: We take our work very seriously, just not ourselves because we love what we do, and do what we love.
2. Honesty: Like any relationship, trust is a key factor to building a loyal and long-lasting connection
3. Ambition: We will go above and beyond to turn your needs into reality
4. Quality: Every decision made is to connect the right person to the right opportunity

Mission statement—this is a short summary: One's main purpose and aim, it often remains unchanged over time. A recruitment company I am a director with has a mission statement of Our mission is to empower people to find the right journey by providing a platform that introduces talent to opportunity. Explains what we do and more importantly why. It also has the overriding objective of the business. A mission statement can be used for more than just business to engage yourself and others.

Standards—you need to document what you do or do not want to have: this could be a certain image, a way of doing certain things, and basically a list of points you all think is important. I'm sure in your personal relationship you would agree honesty is an important part hence when something happens that is dishonest the trust is broken, often never to be fixed. Get clear standards from the get go so everyone is on the same page.

Expectations—what do you expect of yourself, mentors, family members, team, etc. I love using a model Mish taught me. PEP strategy: it stands for purpose, expectation, and progress—it helps keep everyone on the same page.

The two plans I create, then work towards are a business plan and a life plan. I intertwine them together and they run alongside each other. A lot of people I coach either have no plan, a life plan, or maybe just a business plan. I use both because I believe if I treat everything I do the same I have more love for everything I do. Any checkpoints in life will generally coincide with a business goal, that's how I get the most out of myself, I can stay empowered for longer periods of time as there is a purpose behind each achievement.

S-Systems and Structures

What systems are in place to measure progress and performance?

What KPIs are used, and how? Key performance indicators are essential in tracking your results, to see how to improve and what to do next. Depending on your project the KPIs will differ but you still need something to track. Inside our sales business we use KPIs to track work habits, recruitment strategies, sales, development of individuals, tasks that need to be done, and financials. Once you have the information you must use it. Don't be an information hoarder like so many people are. We use KPIs as a measure of performance to benchmark activity and measure productivity.

Lebron James, one of the most skilful NBA players still has his stats recorded during every game: not only is it recorded to help him improve, the information can be used to lift the KPIs for others in the team, and allows the coach to see how everyone works together.

Without goals (hoops) and KPIs (stats) it would be 10 people on a court without any purpose.

"If you can't measure it, you can't improve it"—Peter Drucker.

Sit down with the information that you have collected then use it to enhance your goals as you now have accurate data on what to implement. I use simple documents to track my five-year goals, one-year goals, 90-day challenge, and then a detailed weekly schedule with action points to follow. I reset all my goals when the time frame is up.

What policies and procedures are expected? **Policies and procedures** are designed to influence and determine all major decisions and actions, all activities take place within the boundaries setup. **Procedures** are specific methods employed to express **policies** in action day-to-day to have consistency in the operations of the organisation or individual. It's basically your manual on how to build your dream. This is how we are going to make it happen.

Are there benchmarks of success and manuals to duplicate successful strategies? Once you have a successful strategy write it out so others can copy. If it's in your head and no one else knows the information you will never duplicate yourself. If everything is in your head and not written down that's a lot of wastage of brain power and will not serve you. If you don't have benchmarks for success then research and create some, they are everywhere. If you already know then document it so it can be copied then enhanced. Replication is the key. I love cooking; my fiancé may not agree as she seems to cook more often, it could look like I avoid it. I have a bad strategy when cooking. I get excited, spend hours researching a dish, then prepare a dish, everyone is happy, the crowd is cheering, then two months later when asked about the dish I have no idea where the recipe is or how I made it. On the other hand, my fiancé saves every recipe so if she ever needed to duplicate the recipe, it can be done instantly. Without documentation a successful strategy just doesn't work.

I-Implementation

No matter how good your vision is, how detailed you plan is, without implementation you are screwed. Implementation is what happens, it's what actions, decisions, and processes occur. What systems are used and how? How is the information communicated to your team, or loved ones?

What occurs—what is happening when you are trying to achieve the dream? You have the plan and then you go to implement the plan. You need to know what you are doing then measure against the things you are supposed to be doing. The gap is what's missing, that's the implementation that needs to be done.

When does it happen—when do you take action? Is it during the day, Monday nights from six p.m. to nine p.m., or every Sunday? You need to block out the time you or others will dedicate to the implementation of your plan. Without the time allocated to take action often procrastination happens or you get distracted. Clear action points with weekly time slots will be needed to fulfil outcomes that you're working towards.

Who does it? Who tracks it? How often? You will need to be accountable for your actions and potentially others. For action to happen there needs to be people in place to make it happen. It may be you, family, friends, or colleagues. This is a great opportunity to choose an accountability buddy that inspires you. Send a weekly schedule to your mentor and each week let them know what you did or didn't get done. Work out what percentage of your action points you complete; if you're above 70% most likely you are on track. If you like to gamble or invest maybe use a financial motivation to keep you accountable and stop you from procrastinating.

What evidence is there that the action point is done—how do you know when it has been implemented and completed? What checkpoints will you have in place?

Implementation is the easiest to do but the hardest to be accountable for and the main reason most fail. It is the most important part of the planning process as it's what is getting done versus what is supposed to be getting done, so you can change the actions. The road to success isn't always about what you enjoy but at times it's what pain you are willing to endure. Some want the reward but not the struggle. Some love the victory but not the fight. Taking action will require discipline and challenges will arise. The question you need to ask is what pain am I willing to go through to make my dream a reality?

P-People

What skills do you need to develop to grow to your future self, do you need anyone to help you, a mentor, a team, or can you do it yourself?

My experience is every great person has a bus and fills it with as many people to join them on their journey, having multiple people supporting them will make dreams more likely. Building a great network of people that are living the life, or doing the things you want to be doing is all that's missing to making the dream a reality; remember the circle of five model from Jim Rohn.

Without having a clear success strategy I see many people not able to stick to their dreams for very long which is a shame as you only have one life, there is no dress rehearsal. You deserve to live a life on your terms. Life is hard enough let alone not to be living your dreams.

3) Enjoy the Success/ Enjoy the Ride/ Show Gratitude

People ask me, "Why do you have goals or dreams, do they really work?" If you don't have goals or dreams then it's like being in a walking race or marathon that has no end except for death waiting to take you unexpectedly. I want to celebrate life so I set lots of goals which gives me the opportunity to celebrate as often as I can. Achieving the little outcomes keeps me excited for the big vision.

"Learn how to be happy with what you have while you pursue what you want"—Jim Rohn.

We don't chase dreams to be happy, we are happy and dreams come to us. If you chase a destination for fulfilment it never emerges. Often getting left with discontent. Through my journey I have learnt to celebrate every little success, get enthusiastic with all the small things, and the big things take care of themselves. I learned a long time ago the big successes are few and far between, sometimes a long time between drinks. Keeping myself engaged with the small wins is what keeps me moving forward. Enjoy the ride, for most of us it will be a long one. Every day be thankful for the people in your life who mean something to you or have helped shape you to be the person you are today. Once you can create success/dream/vision for yourself please pass the gift on to others. My gift is taking action. Hopefully yours is inspiring others to live their dream.

Why did I enjoy engineering? It was watching a drawing turn into an immense object, then standing back and admiring what I've created. Why I love entrepreneurship was watching an idea turn into a living, breathing organic business. Why I loved having dreams was I could turn them into a reality. I loved the feeling of solving problems as it gave me a feeling of fulfilment.

This is the strategy I used when I wanted to turn an idea, thought, dream, or drawing into reality. From saving my first $100K, to building multiple businesses, buying the first house, investing into properties, places I wanted to travel to, losing weight, being happy, having purpose.

This is my success strategy.

"Follow your dreams as days are expensive; when you spend a day you have one less day to spend"—Jim Rohn.

Now.

Take action.

CHAPTER 7

Fuck $

1) All Learning Supersedes Money

Australia 1982, just over 5% of the total population had a university degree and now in 2018, we are looking at a marketplace with closer to 30% of the population with a university degree. Commerce 101, if supply and demand is high the marketplace dictates the terms of the pay. It's harder than ever to get a high-paying career. I can imagine if you had a degree in 1982 you probably had a wide spread choice of options, it would have been a candidate's market.

I don't mean let's all rush out and defer your university degrees tomorrow, but you need to be smart about how you decide to play the market. Do you plan on getting any other experiences outside of university? I have conducted hundreds of appointments and interviews over the years with people with degrees or currently studying with their only experience in retail, hospitality, or no experience. The main reason why they didn't have other experience was because they had to concentrate on their studies, or because no one would hire them as they didn't have experience. If it was that important to you, could you get your foot in the door? If it was 1982, concentrating on studies made sense, but now in this market you need to do something different. Looking at the research a large portion of our graduates never work in their studied field. I believe graduates feel a university degree will be enough for them to find their dream career, the research says this ignorance may cost your future.

While writing this book, I've updated my computer three times; it seems impossible that the education system will be able to catch up with the update demand now. I imagine a time coming where halfway through your degree the first few years of learning will be obsolete. The challenge we have now is we have such a fluid workforce you need multiple skills as industries start intertwining, or your skillset needs to be more varied as roles are constantly expanding, especially with the constant changes in technology, the marketplace, and how businesses operate. You need to be multifaceted in workforce and in life.

Therefore, I believe all learning supersedes dollars. It must be the right learning, asking the right questions, spending time with the right people. Two ears and one mouth: if you listen more than you speak you will learn something. I believe the future short courses, specialised mentors, with on-the-job training will be essential with the ever-changing market place. Building skillsets in communication, sales, and technology will be essential for future employees and entrepreneurs.

I was fortunate to build a strong skillset doing commission-only sales which layed a platform for me to build a strong foundation with my mentality, work habits, customer's experience, negotiation skills, sales, everything most companies would love to have in their businesses.

Sales and communication is already one of the most sought-after skills as people still love to buy off people. Technology is an ever-increasing beast which will need people having a better understanding on how it works.

Where do we go from here and what is my point? The skillsets I have built over the years, the discipline I have gained, and the success I have been able to create was from going out to market, fucking up asking questions, finding the right people to build my network, being super proactive with my development, booking in conferences to learn at, workshops to keep building my skillset, constantly learning all areas of my business so I understood how it works from the ground up, sharpening my axe with how I think, constantly challenging the status quo and freshening my mind with new ways of thinking.

I believe the way I built myself will be how the future will need to operate. I don't believe there will be a set training programme that will suit an industry. All information will be relevant for all, with specifics suited for certain fields. With the rise in the transactional economy with businesses like Uber, Airbnb, Airtasker, freelancers, project work, contractors, and having one of the most flexible workforces we have had in Australia's history all looking for independence, flexibility, and more freedom. I can imagine the government's disappointment with tax revenue, so hard to regulate, but they also need to adapt with the changes. A new type of person is slowly being shaped. It's more an entrepreneurial individual having been created out of necessity. I love this as people are slowly becoming more aware but it means we will need to adapt. We have to take action, we can't wait for opportunities to arise, we need to go after what we want. With the creation of LinkedIn it has never been easier. What does your resume and experience say about you? Everyone online now has access to millions of resumes in Australia. We need to sharpen our axe today.

2) Relationship With $

Growing up I hated millionaires, I didn't really know what a millionaire was but all the same I disliked them, I had never met one but I still judged. Was it because I envied them? Maybe it was the general conversation with people I surrounded myself with where they blamed them for their misfortunes. They were the lucky ones that were born into wealth. They had it easy. I assumed that they must've got to where they were because they were ripping someone off. So my relationship with money early on was it wasn't okay to make lots of money as that would be showing off, what would people say about me? If I did have money would others try and take advantage of me?

It wasn't until my early twenties that I came across my first millionaire: it was working in my first business, a network-marketing business, he had a very open and honest conversation with me. He told me how hard he worked, he had a similar upbringing to me, he was normal, and he stressed the importance of building communication/sales skills. He mentioned the work he now does in the community, how he lives his life. I felt inspired and a sense of freedom and purpose consumed me. I realised I had a bad relationship with money, not with millionaires.

So many of us feel we don't deserve an abundance of money! Why the fuck not? We have the same amount of time in the day as everyone else, we have opportunities like everyone else, but what are we going to do? Blame others? Feel sorry for ourselves? Hope it will change one day?

Success changes people, I agree; with the individuals I've met it has always been for the better, to enrich their and others' lives, with choices they can have a wider impact on people.

Would you like to lean in and play a game to feel what your wealth blueprint is?

Now this is a feeling-based activity for you to understand your relationship with money from an internal aspect.

It may seem like I've gone completely fucking crazy but bear with me.

Go to a quiet place and I encourage you to start to breathe deep into your belly and feel what your gut is telling you; this will invoke your intuition which lies deep in your gut. Intuition is your inner compass, it tells you when you're in line or if there is something to be wary of. Intuition only knows what your mind is saying. Remembering your body will believe your thoughts as your mind has convinced the body it's real.

Now you have started to breathe deep ask the question to yourself: what is my annual worth? What is the monetary figure I should be paid each year? Start at $10,000 and go up by $10,000 increments and really feel when it starts to get uncomfortable. When the figure becomes uncomfortable that's when you know what you believe you're worth.

As an example, I did this exercise with a colleague of mine and at $40,000 he had the comfortable feeling and then got uncomfortable when I went above that figure. He was receiving $80,000 a year in revenue and was wondering why it was so challenging holding onto the money he was generating. If you don't change the internal belief you have around money you will never hold onto it for long, even if you keep getting paid more.

It was an activity I did early on to understand: what I felt I was worth. I completely undervalued myself. I would be interested to hear how you matched up. If you overvalued yourself test your worth on the open market; you may be overconfident or you may be worth more. If you have undervalued yourself maybe you need to look at building some new skills around belief strategies, confidence with money, salesmanship, or any other workshops that would help you create value of yourself again.

3) Don't Choose Short-Term Results, Play The Long Game

The Marshmallow Experiment

The experiment began by bringing each child into a private room, sitting them down in a chair, and placing a marshmallow on the table in front of them. At this point, the researcher offered a deal to the child. The researcher told the child that he was going to leave the room and that if the child did not eat the marshmallow while he was away, then they would be rewarded with a second marshmallow. However, if the child decided to eat the first one before the researcher came back, then they would not get a second marshmallow. So the choice was simple: one treat right now or two treats later. The researcher left the room for 15 minutes. As you can imagine, the footage of the children waiting alone in the room was rather entertaining. Some kids jumped up and ate the first marshmallow as soon as the researcher closed the door. Others wiggled and bounced and scooted in their chairs as they tried to restrain themselves, but eventually gave in to temptation a few minutes later. And finally, a few of the children did manage to wait the entire time.

The researchers followed each child for more than 40 years and over and over again, the group who waited patiently for the second marshmallow succeeded in whatever capacity they were measuring. In other words, this series of experiments proved that the ability to delay gratification was critical for success in life.

Success usually comes down to choosing the pain of discipline over the ease of distraction. And that's exactly what delayed gratification is all about.

The marshmellow test was conducted In the 1960s, by a Stanford professor named Walter Mischel whom began conducting a series of important psychological studies. During his experiments, Mischel and his team tested hundreds of children—most of them around the ages of four and five years old—and revealed what is now believed to be one of the most important characteristics for success in health, work, and life.

I often see individuals choose opportunities based on what will give them money for tomorrow versus what will make them happy/fulfilled in one, five, 10, or 20 years. The answer I always get is "Well, I don't know what I want." The older you get the harder it is to change as your financial obligations increase; the earlier you plug in the quicker you will have clarity. It's never too late to change. Mistakes I have made are: I will stay at this job so I can fund a holiday that will make me feel good; I can't do an internship at a major company as how will I fund my weekend drinking which I need to make me feel good; I get paid well here so I don't need to change as I have a pretty good life after work. My advice is simple: dont waste your time if it doesn't have a long-term purpose attached.

Questions I ask to give myself clarity with decision making:

Remembering around 70% of all humans' decisions will be based on emotion so the questions I asked are based around the feelings I would want to have then deciding on how to make it happen.

If you were to have the same emotions every day for the next five years what emotions would you want to feel?

List your top three goals in the next five years; what feelings are you hoping the goal will give you?

Based on what you are currently doing, what emotions are you experiencing and what emotions will you experience in the next five years?

What do you need to add into your life? What do you need to remove to start getting you feeling the way you need to so the outcomes can happen?

4) You Will Retire, When Are You Going To Think About It?

The average life expectancy for Australians if they retire at 65 is just over 21 years. The longer you live the better your average life expectancy becomes. For example, if you reach the average life expectancy that you had at 65, that is, you reach the age of 86, then you can expect to live another six or so years. The average life expectancy for Australians will be closer to 91 years old. If you retire before the age of 65, and many Australians do, then you can expect a potential retirement time of more than 21 years.

The advancements in the medical field and with technology forever changing, we will live longer. The problem with living longer is with the retirement pension. Most of us younger than 40 were expecting to receive the pension, the chances are it will be obsolete. There are already talks of a means test about who will qualify to receive benefits. Based on data from the last nine years the retirement ages in Australia have increased by two years from 65-67 years old and research points towards 70 years old in the near future. The average superannuation people are retiring on is around $214,000. The numbers don't add up. Even if you do own your house and live on average of 21 years based on the current numbers, it's living off $195.97 per person per week. That's less than $200 to cover your weekly living expenses.

Now that's a fucking scary thought.

You'll need to financially support yourself for over 21 years, with life expectancy increasing, the money needed will have to be significantly higher. I'm not even looking at factoring inflation in right now but I imagine even having a million dollars in super will give you less than minimum wage once you retire. I imagine all over the Western world figures would point towards massive challenges with an ever-ageing population. Even right now in Australia there are large percentages of retirees living on minimum wage.

The point I'm making is you can't afford to keep making short-terms decisions; if you don't focus on retirement now you will be fucked as it's coming whether you like it or not.

5) You Will Die, When Are You Going to Think About It?

Then you die ...

How would you want to be remembered? At some point there may be a legacy you want to leave behind that's generally the ego expressing the need but if it's important go crazy. Do you want to be remembered for the book you wrote, how happy you are, how you loved your family, the legacy you built while you were alive that will be passed down the generations? Or do you want to be remembered as a selfish fuck that only thought of themselves, you never made time for the right people and you complained about everything in your life?

Are people a better version of themselves around you? #yolo you only live once, there is no time to waste. If you fucked up don't worry about it, make amends in areas you can control. Time isn't on our side. I'm by far not perfect but I can be happy that I use death as a motivation to make people around me feel good. Today is all we have, we never know if tomorrow will come. One of my favourite bars has a classic sign inside—'Free beer tomorrow'. Every time I walk in tomorrow never seems to come.

When you're young you think you're invincible and will live forever. Jumping off roofs, thinking you are a professional stuntman, nothing seems to worry you, and as you get older you are wary. Then you experience the death of a friend, loved one, and it all changes; you realise that we aren't immortal. I remember my granddad passed away; I wasn't close to him, I was very young, and it was the first funeral I ever went to, everything seemed to change from that point. Death seems inevitable instead of a distant ultra-reality. I imagine the emotions being more heightened with a close family member or friend.

Why do you put things off? You could die tomorrow, you never know when the grim reaper is going to be tapping on your shoulder and it's your turn.

So many people don't have urgency and immediacy around taking action on the dreams they have always wanted to do now. Free beer tomorrow. It can't wait. You need to act today.

Have you made peace with death? It's coming for you if you like it or not. What is it you wanted to do before you die? Everyone talks about leaving a legacy, yes, great it will give you purpose for today and for the future. Living for today is the greatest legacy you can leave and empower so many people around you. Don't wait; live the life you dream of today through the emotions you want to have, around the people you want to be around, and have your dream outcomes.

Take action today ... don't wait.

6) Belief About $

Living in Sydney all I hear about is how house prices are so expensive; when I travel I notice people asking, "Where are you from?" then when I tell them "Sydney" they say, "Oh, that's expensive." Now I hear myself telling everyone, "Sydney is expensive."

I can see the fucking problem everyone is creating: 1) we are pushing house prices up by justifying it's expensive and all agreeing to pay the price and 2) what chances do the next generation have with this attitude we are creating which is basically saying you have zero chance to ever buy a house.

Growing up in Perth I had the same problem. Everyone talked about how expensive Perth is, houses are hard to buy, prices keep going up, so my belief was well, what chance will I have to buy a house? It was in my subconscious, it was something I wasn't actively thinking about but it was ingrained into my head from a young age.

I'm guessing wherever in the world you go the same conversations are probably being had.

The issue is I now have a belief, that I will never be able to create the income needed to buy a house; right or wrong, the belief is ingrained in me and hard to change.

It wasn't until my late twenties when I was introduced to a mortgage broker that was my turning point; he explained to me how the system worked, he mapped out a pathway on what I needed to achieve if I was to buy a property, he followed the Daniel Tonkin strategy without him knowing. It didn't seem as hard as everyone made it out to be. I was then able to shake off my beliefs and start purchasing property. Imagine if I had a different belief system from a younger age or access to people who could educate me versus listening to people complain and talk about what they think they know on a subject.

Often people we think are helping us are doing us an injustice accidentally. The same with shares, crypto-currencies and so on: it wasn't until I sat down with an expert that they explained to me how it works, how to get started and then I was truly able to decide on what I wanted to do with my money. It's funny when talking about investing in something new, people often mention a story they heard from Auntie Helga's cousin Harry who knew a guy that lost $50K in crypto-currency, that's a bad investment, stay away. It's no different to the house market. It's no different to the importance people have on money mentioning it's hard to come by so you need to save, save, save. Yes, savings are important, yes, people have done silly things with money so they may not have it. If you have a belief system built around not having any you will struggle to attract abundance.

What was your conditioning growing up to form your current beliefs? Money was often mentioned in my household as I grew up, money is probably mentioned in most households all the time. Again, every negative conversation you have with people regarding money is just building on your belief system that it's hard to find. Your mind will give you what you think and talk about.

Imagine our future children growing up conditioned that the cost of owning a house is too high and will be impossible to buy; if you don't go to university you won't be able to live a good life; you need to get a good job to grow, not a shit one. All these conditionings are making it harder and harder for others to build their dreams. I'm not saying it's going to be easy but there are so many ways of making a dream become a reality, especially in today's market. At least give everyone a chance to dream without corruption and give them education from experts so they can make an educated decision based on realties not theories, thoughts, or second-hand information.

7) Never Too Late to Change

Age is in your mind; you are never too young, never too old to start on your dream.

This book is for everyone at all ages, it's a reminder it's never too early or late to start. Doesn't matter what you want to do, dream big. I opened my company as a 22-year-old, I had no money, no real experience, and most people I was doing appointments to work with me were older than me but I had to start somewhere and I'm glad I didn't apply all the advice people would offer when discussing my dreams. I listened and decided what I wanted to do based on me not what other people were saying because with all the things to consider I would've never got started. I would've waited for the perfect age, the perfect amount of money, the perfect people, the perfect client. It never works out that way. Make the jump, but if you do, get a mentor.

Here are a few great examples of individuals that are super young and had success or were able to attain success later on in life in a variety of ways, and everyone has a different dream. It just shows, don't give up on your dream and it's never too early or too late to start, the perfect time is now.

Joan of Arc, a peasant girl living in medieval France, believed that God had chosen her to lead France to victory in its long-running war with England. With no military training, Joan convinced the embattled crown prince Charles of Valois to allow her to lead a French army to the besieged city of Orléans, where it achieved a momentous victory over the English and their French allies, the Burgundians. After seeing the prince crowned King Charles VII, Joan was 18 years old.

Harland Sanders, better known as Colonel Sanders, was 62 when he franchised Kentucky Fried Chicken in 1952, which he would sell for $US2 million 12 years later.

Harry Bernstein spent a long life writing in obscurity, achieving notoriety at long last at age 96 for his 2007 memoir *The Invisible Wall: A Love Story That Broke Barriers.*

An Australian adventurer I recently read an article about was Queensland teen Alyssa Azar who has succeeded in her bid to become the youngest Australian in history to scale Mount Everest. After two previous attempts, this time her climb went without a hitch. In a message posted on her Facebook page, the 19-year-old's achievement was verified. Adventure has been a major part of Ms Azar's life since she was eight, when she completed her first challenge, crossing the Kokoda Track in Papua New Guinea. She has also completed treks such as Everest Base Camp, Mount Kosciuszko, Mount Kilimanjaro, and the Aussie 10—the highest peaks in Australia.

The last takeout is when you start to follow your dream don't just lead with the head, you need to lead with the heart. When you are coming from a heart space people feel what you are saying; this philosophy changed my life and career and took it to a whole new level. For years I just used my head, I was out of touch with what I was feeling. Once I opened the space this was the final piece of the missing puzzle. Every mentor I was working with had one thing in common, they had a huge heart which drove their mind to achieve. Connect the mind to the heart and you will be a force to be reckoned with.

As soon as you settle you stop growing and death ends up being a waiting game as it's always imminent.

Use your time.

CHAPTER 8

Live Happily Ever After

The finishing line is near and before we end our journey together I would love to share some of my philosophies; as I start to share my philosophies with you, I imagine you will begin to think about your own. That's the whole idea of this chapter, for you to expand on what's important to you, change the way you view everyday life especially what seems to be the boring bits, and finally what you will stand for. The purpose of this chapter is to help shape your way of thinking to get you ready to start taking action with the final word of our book. We are entering the final phase; I encourage you to borrow my ideas or recreate your own.

1) Live Every Day Like It's Your Last

Nothing better than starting the weekend with a great romantic comedy which leaves you on the brink of tears!

My fiancé's favourite movie is About Time. It's a heartfelt movie that reminds you what's important in life. Tim the main character is a clumsy young adult that can time travel. An ability he has inherited from his dad. Tim finds the love of his life and spends a lot of energy going back in time trying to fix past problems.

At the end of the movie Tim asks his dad, "How do you get through life?" He answers, "I live every day normally, then travel back in time to repeat the day, this time taking notice of all the beauty."

At the end of the movie Tim explains he has learnt his final lesson from time travel. At this point Tim has a lovely family with the girl of his dreams. He explains that he doesn't time travel at all anymore, he lives every day like he deliberately came back to that day to enjoy the final day of his extraordinary ordinary life.

I know it's a movie but what great lessons it has in it. We are all travelling through time together every day of our lives, all we can do is enjoy the ride.

If you were to live life every day as if it were your last what mindset or actions would you take?

2) Create Your Home Feel

The first thing I do when I get home is take off my jacket, then tie, shoes, followed by socks, shirt, and lastly trousers. If it's hot I just wear my underwear (if people are around, shorts, if they aren't close friends, maybe a t shirt). If it's cold I get the comfiest track pants and hand-knitted jumper on and ready for a big night of cooking, eating, drinking wine, laughing, talking, and watching movies. The feeling I create when doing these actions makes me feel like home, it's what I love doing, I'm content, relaxed, and I find it easy to be myself.

I want my home to feel warm, inspiring, safe, creative, fun, and have a family feel, everyone who is a part of the house plays a role with the decorating and creating their own space. My aim is to create a family feel with every tribe I'm a part of: workshops, work, sports team, friendship groups, art classes, anywhere that I'm building a community. All families are weird and wacky; I'm yet to meet a normal family. The imperfections are what makes the relationships unique. Everyone has a different upbringing and some maybe not the ideal family situation but it's about that family feel that you want to create with the tribes you spend time with.

What does home feel mean to me?

Laughing as much as I can, creating awkward situations, having intense conversations about random topics, arguing about things that are irrelevant, showing love to each other, having an artistic creative aspect, sticking up for each other, caring for one another, growing with one another, supporting each other, making each other a better version of themselves, not putting each other down, making time for each other, trying not to use each other as a punching bag (try), talking about life, sharing our dreams, having a common purpose, being hungry but humble, challenging one other, farting in front of each other, seeing each other at our worse, then also at our best, and last of all sharing the love.

The more environments you create with this feel, the more empowered you will be and you will bring tribes of people with you on your journey.

What does home feel like to you?

How can you bring those feelings into your tribes and environments?

3) Have Fun

Don't take yourself so seriously, you can take your work, life, projects seriously but not yourself.

You will spend a lot of time at work so enjoy it or find a place you can, you will spend a lot of time with your family, you can't change your family but you can influence them, so enjoy it. Do not die of terminal seriousness; if you're going to get serious about something, get serious about your happiness and what's important to you.

What makes you laugh?

Can you do more of it?

4) Do Shit You Love

The older you get the more you prioritise the things you want to do. Be careful not to confuse wants and loves. I love the beach and even though its across from where I live I often find myself wanting to sit on the lounge, thinking that is so comfy and I can't be bothered moving as I'm tired. We often get caught in these traps that allow us to feel nothing; it's a zombie-like state and we get caught up in procrastination. The longer we sit the more we get caught up in our thoughts or distracted by TV or phones that hypnotise us from what's happening around us, even though we know deep down if we were at the beach or doing something we love we would be feeling fresh, free, and inspired. Doing things you love re-energises you instantly; don't get left on the couch to ponder life, live it.

When I'm in my thoughts I often ponder about tomorrow, or the past, I very rarely use to live in the now.

My spiritual journey has got me out of my head by using techniques like yoga, meditation, and doing shit I love. It allows me to get out of my head and live life right now.

What shit do you love?

Are you making a conscious effort to do it on a weekly basis or does it just happen?

5) Creating Positive Change

Have you woken up and snoozed your alarm four to five times before you finally got up? Have you ever walked outside and complained about the weather being too hot, cold, or rainy? On the way to work under your breath whispered profanities about the traffic being bad, the train being delayed, or the bus driver nearly killing you multiple times with his terrible driving? Finally arrived at work and all you can do is visualise the exact time you will be leaving, then your manager gives you loads of work and you know you will need to stay back? Called in sick because you couldn't be fucked going in to work, a party, or a family outing?

Imagine if this was in reverse? Would that change anything about how you go about your day-to-day life? Would it change people's experiences when they are around you? Or do you think those actions are normal and everyone does it so it's okay?

I will be the first to put my hand up and say, "Yes, all those funny experiences were me." From time to time I still have the urge to fall back into the negativity trap. But I want to create a positive change so it starts with YOU. If you want to create positive change in yourself and others you need to be positive yourself. Where does it start?

The hardest ones to fix are the ones in denial about their mindset, they believe they are positive but everyone else isn't; if you read this with the mindset of yes I want to create positive change you will improve your state by just accepting you have a part of you to work on.

First write down the moments that you feel unmotivated or uninspired?

What are the moments that you think are normal but probably have an impact on your state of mind in a negative way and frustration keeps creeping in?

What steps do you want to take to move forward?

Who will help you stay on track?

My last point is if you want to creative positive change choose the things you want to give a fuck about. If you want to have a great day why snooze your alarm four to five times? If you don't want to get frustrated then why focus on how bad traffic is? If you care about your children, great, give a fuck about them, don't get caught up that they ate the last ice cream in the freezer and you told them multiple times not to. Priorities seem completely off. Positive change only happens when you focus on positive outcomes.

6) Nothing Is Perfect, Perfection Is an Illusion

I remember the day I picked up my brand-new Audi A4; it was the first time I could afford to purchase a brand-new car. The feeling I had was immense excitement, proud and a feeling of accomplishment as it had been a dream of mine for some time. I remember walking into the Audi dealership in Five Dock and picking up my new set of keys, walking around the car, checking every nook and cranny, before getting in the car to take the Audi on its maiden voyage; it was perfect in every way. I jumped into the car, put my favourite song on, played it as loud as I could, opened the sunroof, and proceeded to drive. I didn't want to stop, I kept driving all over Sydney; I went to Bondi, Manly, Cronulla, I could've driven all day. When I finally got home I wanted to have a last sweep of the car and have a look again at every nook and cranny. I noticed brake dust on the rims, dust settling its way over the black car already, and a massive white bird shit on the roof. I was instantly distraught at what happened to my idea of perfection. Chasing perfection only gives you a very short-lived feeling as perfection never lasts.

I have had perfect days when it's been sunny and perfect days when it's been rainy; perfection is an illusion that can't be maintained and has sent the best of us crazy. Aim to do your best, not to be perfect. Every day as you grow your ideal perfection will change so it will never be met. Strive to do your best as the journey is what matters, not the final destination. You will be on the journey longer than you will able to appreciate the destination as the emotions of arriving won't last long until it becomes a part of your life. If you don't love the journey you will feel unfulfilled at the destination.

The imperfections are what makes us beautiful but ordinary. I invite you to find spelling mistakes as I'm sure there will be a few, these mistakes humanise us; I know in one year when I read back through this book, as I've learnt and grown as a person, there will be changes I would want to make but right now the book is exactly what I want to share based on the information I have collected in the last 32 years, so I'm at peace with that. No need to let fear overcome me, no time to let anxiety overcome my thoughts or get depressed about the past. I'm just enjoying writing this book, overlooking the ocean on beautiful North Stradbroke Island, watching the occasional whale swim past, walking to the beach, swimming a few times a day, eating amazing food, and hanging with friends I've known for years. If only one person takes action on the points from my book it was worth writing, even if that one person is me.

From an ordinary successful guy

Now we are entering the final phase of the book! Game face on. Let's get ready to take action ...

The Final Word
Before you check out this is your opportunity to take action.

Isn't it about time you take action?

Are you waiting for permission?

PERMISSION GRANTED!

What the fuck are you waiting for? Christmas, winter, death, future: it's all coming regardless of what you do!

Draw a line in the sand and from this point on take action on your dreams, vision, outcomes, and most importantly YOUR LIFE!!!

Don't do what I did for years and wait for everything to be completely broken, destroyed, or fucked before I felt it necessary to take action.

What do you need to learn?

What action do you need to take?

What action points will you start from today?

As soon as you have written them down have dates, times allocated, and then take action.

Thanks for sharing the journey with me, it's been an amazing ride! I look forward to hearing how everyone is implementing aspects of my book to their everyday life.

I want to know how shit happens! Then rainbows are happening in your lives so feel free to email me any stories you want to share.

If you want to get in contact with me my email address is Daniel@shithappensthenrainbows.com.au

From the expert of taking action and killer of procrastination

The successful ordinary guy,
Daniel Tonkin

Acknowledgments

Wow, where to start!! There have been so many people who have helped shape my life and are the reasons I'm here today!

The book was a huge, messy thing that required more than my experiences to shape.

First and foremost, thank you to my beautiful fiancé and wife-to-be, Emily. Not only do you whip me into gear when I start doubting but you are my rock. Not only do you make me a better person, but your unconditional love and constant feedback was essential for helping this project come together. I love you.

To Ava, my beautiful daughter, when you came into my life my perception on the world changed forever. You gave me a new purpose which I will be forever grateful for. I love you and this book would not have been possible without you.

I have to say thanks to Dave Thompson who believed in me enough to share my journey, experiences, and lessons. I've always wanted to stay humble while writing, so thank you for showing me how to be true to myself and get my message out to the world. You gave me the opportunity to make this happen, I will be forever grateful.

Thanks to the crew at the Inspirational Book Writers Retreat that helped me through writer's block. My book has taken me years to get to this stage, thanks for helping me get over the finish line.

Now I want to say thanks to my heroes.

My mum, thanks for putting up with the shit I caused in my early years, you are such a hard worker and showed me you can achieve the things you love by sticking to what you want. I love you.

My step-dad Calvin, who took me into his house at such a young age, you were a great role model for me growing up even if I didn't show gratitude. Thank you for helping me become the man I am today.

My dad for helping me see the world in a different way, you gave me huge motivation very early on to grab life by the balls and make things happen or I could get left behind.

To my mother in law Helen, what an amazing human you are, not only giving birth to my amazing wife to be, but for spending hours reading my book, giving me feedback and making sure my voice was still prevalent through the book.

My auntie Karen, the most positive person I know. Such a can-do attitude and helped me so much in my early years as an entrepreneur, gave me massive belief, I thank you.

My grandad who loves us dearly, so much so he jumped in the pool fully clothed if we did our homework. Was an inspiration to me before I knew what inspiration was. The first entrepreneur I knew. Thank you for changing my life for the better.

To Tu-tu whom passed away before the book was published, Wow! what a life you have lived. You have always been a supporter of mine. Even one of my first customers in my first business. I'm truly grateful to have spent time with you. you will be remembered forever. I love you.

Thank you to my daughter's mother, Rachel; such an amazing mother to my daughter and still such a supporter for what I'm doing.

Must say a massive thanks to my four mentors who made the biggest impact on my life, then helped me get my businesses to take flight!

Acknowledgments

1) Farid Lerno

2) Darren Wright

3) Steve Sapsford

4) Michele Jones

You all came into my life at different times throughout my career. Farid Lerno, you were the one who put me on the map, changed my beliefs about what I can do with my life, with not just living a life but owning your life. You are the one that opened my mind to entrepreneurship, started me on my journey to achieve my dreams. Darren, my next mentor, helped me turn from being a rebel without a cause to a young adult ready to take on the world. Steve came into my life next and shaped me to be a young professional. Mish, who had the biggest impact on my life, helped me not only take my business to the next level, helped me love again, trust again, and gave me the resources to make this book come to life.

Jenny Lam, wow, what an inspiration! I met you as a 19-year-old, it has been my absolute pleasure mentoring you over the last nine years; watching you develop into such a successful entrepreneur, friend, and all-round superstar made me realise I do have a message to share and I can have an impact on the world. Hopefully you win Masterchef 2018!!

My three best friends whom I see as family: Ryan, Brenden, and Rory! You have all been a massive part in my life. Ryan, I've learnt love from, Brenden, trust, and Rory, how to be happy all the time; even when I try and fuck with his head he is still the happiest person I know. All three of you are such an inspiration, thank you.

I have to send some love to Sasha Mihajlovic and Travis Armour. They both introduced me to my first business opportunities which shaped me to who I am today.

To everyone else who has had such an impact in my life and helped me become the man I am today, from my office staff at STM, business partners at Wow, every contractor in our organisation, every mentor who has shaped my thinking, friends, and family.

Finally, to the readers that will decide to read my book. No, I'm not a writer, yes, there will be mistakes. I've spent hundreds of hours getting this ready for you. Thank you for taking the time to read. Yes, if you take action you will live a life on your terms.

I guess now I am a writer, an author, and an ordinary successful guy!

Much love,
Daniel Tonkin.

About The Author

Daniel Tonkin is an ordinary successful guy, he is an entrepreneur, father, son, brother, husband to be, mentor, friend and all round good guy.

He owns 3 companies that generate millions of dollars in revenue each year.

This is his journey of how business saved his life.

This is the story of how entrepreneurship taught Daniel the lessons in happiness, that it's about taking action no matter how small each day.

Contact Daniel Tonkin

Private Mentoring

I work with a small, exclusive number of private mentoring clients to help you build your business, and achieve your dreams.

To find out more, email me:
daniel@shithappensthenrainbows.com.au

Speaking

If the message in this book resonates with your organisation, I can also be hired for speaking engagements.

To find out more, email me:
daniel@shithappensthenrainbows.com.au

Media/Other Enquiries

For all other enquiries, including media, and bulk book sales, please email me:
daniel@shithappensthenrainbows.com.au

www.ingramcontent.com/pod-product-compliance
Lightning Source LLC
Chambersburg PA
CBHW020438220526
45464CB00002B/759